the Characters in Pilgrim's Progress

**Whyte's classic and compelling
exposition of Bunyan's immortal
PILGRIM'S PROGRESS**

Alexander Whyte

D1430850

BAKER BOOK HOUSE
Grand Rapids, Michigan

Formerly published under the title,
Bunyan Characters

Paperback edition issued 1976
by Baker Book House

ISBN: 0-8010-9510-7

PHOTOLITHOPRINTED BY CUSHING - MALLOY, INC.
ANN ARBOR, MICHIGAN, UNITED STATES OF AMERICA
1976

CONTENTS

CONTENTS

I

INTRODUCTORY

'The express image' [*Gr,* 'the character'].—*Heb.* i. 3.

THE word 'character' occurs only once in the New Testament, and that is in the passage in the prologue of the Epistle to the Hebrews, where the original word is translated 'express image' in our version. Our Lord is the Express Image of the Invisible Father. No man hath seen God at any time. The only-begotten Son, who is in the bosom of the Father, He hath declared Him. The Father hath sealed His divine image upon His Son, so that he that hath seen the Son hath seen the Father. The Son is thus the Father's character stamped upon and set forth in human nature. The Word was made flesh. This is the highest and best use to which our so expressive word 'character' has ever been put, and the use to which it is put when we speak of Bunyan's Characters partakes of the same high sense and usage. For it is of the outstanding good or evil in a man that we think when we speak of his character. It is really either of his likeness or unlikeness to Jesus Christ we speak, and then, through Him, his likeness or unlikeness to God Himself.

And thus it is that the adjective 'moral' usually accompanies our word ' character '—moral or immoral. A man's character does not have its seat or source in his body; character is not a physical thing: not even in his mind; it is not an intellectual thing. Character comes up out of the will and out of the heart. There are more good minds, as we say, in the world than there are good hearts. There are more clever people than good people; character,—high, spotless, saintly character,—is a far rarer thing in this world than talent or even genius. Character is an infinitely better thing than either of these, and it is of corresponding rarity. And yet so true is it that the world loves its own, that all men worship talent, and even bodily strength and bodily beauty, while only one here and one there either understands or values or pursues moral character, though it is the strength and the beauty and the sweetness of the soul.

We naturally turn to Bishop Butler when we think of moral character. Butler is an author who has drawn no characters of his own. Butler's genius was not creative like Shakespeare's or Bunyan's. Butler had not that splendid imagination which those two masters in character-painting possessed, but he had very great gifts of his own, and he has done us very great service by means of his gifts. Bishop Butler has helped many men in the intelligent formation of their character, and what higher praise could be given to any author? Butler will lie on our table all winter beside Bunyan; the bishop beside the tinker, the philosopher beside the poet, the moralist beside the evangelical minister.

In seeking a solid bottom for our subject, then,

we naturally turn to Butler. Bunyan will people the house for us once it is built, but Butler lays bare for us the naked rock on which men like Bunyan build and beautify and people the dwelling-place of God and man. What exactly is this thing, character, we hear so much about? we ask the sagacious bishop. And how shall we understand our own character so as to form it well till it stands firm and endures? 'Character,' answers Butler, in his bald, dry, deep way, 'by character is meant that temper, taste, disposition, whole frame of mind from whence we act in one way rather than another . . . those principles from which a man acts, when they become fixed and habitual in him we call his character. . . . And consequently there is a far greater variety in men's characters than there is in the features of their faces.' Open Bunyan now, with Butler's keywords in your mind, and see the various tempers, tastes, dispositions, frames of mind from which his various characters act, and which, at bottom, really make them the characters, good or bad, which they are. See the principles which Bunyan has with such inimitable felicity embodied and exhibited in their names, the principles within them from which they have acted till they have become a habit and then a character, that character which they themselves are and will remain. See the variety of John Bunyan's characters, a richer and a more endless variety than are the features of their faces. Christian and Christiana, Obstinate and Pliable, Mr. Fearing and Mr. Feeblemind, Temporary and Talkative, Mr. Byends and Mr. Facing-both-ways, Simple, Sloth, Presumption, that brisk lad Ignorance, and the genuine Mr. Brisk himself. And then Captain Boasting, Mr. High-mind, Mr. Wet-Eyes, and so on, through a less known (but equally well worth knowing) company of municipal and military characters in the *Holy War*.

We shall see, as we proceed, how this and that character in Bunyan was formed and deformed. But let us ask in this introductory lecture if we can find out any law or principle upon which all our own characters, good or bad, are formed. Do our characters come to be what they are by chance, or have we anything to do in the formation of our own characters, and if so, in what way? And here, again, Butler steps forward at our call with his key to our own and to all Bunyan's characters in his hand, and in three familiar and fruitful words he answers our question and gives us food for thought and solemn reflection for a lifetime. There are but three steps, says Butler, from earth to heaven, or, if you will, from earth to hell—acts, habits, character. All Butler's prophetic burden is bound up in these three great words—acts, habits, character. Remember and ponder these three words, and you will in due time become a moral philosopher. Ponder and practise them, and you will become what is infinitely better—a moral man. For acts, often repeated, gradually become habits, and habits, long enough continued, settle and harden and solidify into character. And thus it is that the severe and laconic bishop has so often made us shudder as he demonstrated it to us that we are all with our own hands shaping our character not only for this world, but much more for the world to come, by every act we perform, by every word we speak, almost by every breath we draw. Butler is one of the most terrible authors in the world. He stands on our nearest shelf with Dante on one side of him and Pascal on the other. He is indeed terrible, but it is with a terror that purifies the heart and keeps the life in the hour of temptation. Paul sometimes arms himself with the same terror; only he composes in another style than that of Butler, and, with all his vivid intensity, he calls it the terror of the Lord. Paul and Bunyan are of the same school of moralists and stylists; Butler went to school to the Stoics, to Aristotle, and to Plato.

Our Lord Himself came to be the express image He was and is by living and acting under this same universal law of human life—acts, habits, character. He was made perfect on this same principle. He learned obedience both by the things that He did, and the things that He suffered. Butler says in one deep place, that benevolence and justice and veracity are the basis of all good character in God and in man, and thus also in the God-man. And those three foundation stones of our Lord's character settled deeper and grew stronger to bear and to suffer as He went on practising acts and speaking words of justice, goodness, and truth. And so of all the other elements of His moral character. Our Lord left Gethsemane a much more submissive and a much more surrendered man than He entered it. His forgiveness of injuries, and thus His splendid benevolence, had not yet come to its climax and crown till He said on the cross,

'Father, forgive them. And, as He was, so are we
in this world. This world's evil and ill-desert made
it but the better arena and theatre for the develop-
ment and the display of His moral character; and
the same instruments that fashioned Him into the
perfect and express image He was and is, are still,
happily, in full operation. Take that divinest and
noblest of all instruments for the carving out and
refining of moral character, the will of God. How
our Lord made His own unselfish and unsinful will
to bow to silence and to praise before the holy will
of His Father, till that gave the finishing touch to
His always sanctified will and heart! And, happily,
that awful and blessed instrument for the formation
of moral character is still active and available to those
whose ambition rises to moral character, and who
are aiming at heaven in all they do and all they
suffer upon the earth. Gethsemane has gone out
till it has covered all the earth. Its cup, if not in
all the depth and strength of its first mixture, still
in quite sufficient bitterness, is put many times in
life into every man's hand. There is not a day,
there is not an hour of the day, that the disciple of
the submissive and all-surrendered Son has not the
opportunity to say with his Master, If it be possible,
let this cup pass : nevertheless, not as I will, but as
Thou wilt.

It is not in the great tragedies of life only that
character is tested and strengthened and consolidated. No man who is not himself under God's
moral and spiritual instruments could believe how
often in the quietest, clearest, and least tempest-
uous day he has the chance and the call to say, Yea,

Lord, Thy will be done. And, then, when the confessedly tragic days and nights come, when all men admit that this is Gethsemane indeed, the practised soul is able, with a calmness and a peace that confound and offend the bystanders, to say, to act so that he does not need to say, Not my will, but Thine. And so of all the other forms and features of moral character; so of humility and meekness, so of purity and temperance, so of magnanimity and munificence, so of all self-suppression and self-extinction, and all corresponding exalting and magnifying and benefiting of other men. Whatever other passing uses this present world, so full of trial and temptation and suffering, may have, this surely is the supreme and final use of it—to be a furnace, a graving-house, a refining place for human character. Literally all things in this life and in this world—I challenge you to point out a single exception—work together for this supreme and only good, the purification, the refining, the testing, and the approval of human character. Not only so, but we are all in the very heat of the furnace, and under the very graving iron and in the very refining fire that our prefigured and predestinated character needs. Your life and its trials would not suit the necessities of my moral character, and you would lose your soul beyond redemption if you exchanged lots with me. You do not put a pearl under the potter's wheel; you do not cast clay into a refining fire. Abraham's character was not like David's, nor David's like Christ's, nor Christ's like Paul's. As Butler says, there is 'a providential disposition of things' around every one of us, and it is as exactly suited to the flaws and excrescences, the faults and corruptions of our character as if Providence had had no other life to make a disposition of things for but one, and that one our own. Have you discovered that in your life, or any measure of that? Have you acknowledged to God that you have at last discovered the true key of your life? Have you given Him the satisfaction to know that He is not making His providential dispositions around a stock or a stone, but that He has one under His hand who understands His hand, and responds to it, and rises up to meet and salute it?

And we cease to wonder so much at the care God takes of human character, and the cost He lays out upon it, when we think that it is the only work of His hands that shall last for ever. It is fit, surely, that the ephemeral should minister to the eternal, and time to eternity, and all else in this world to the only thing in this world that shall endure and survive this world. All else we possess and pursue shall fade and perish, our moral character shall alone survive. Riches, honours, possessions, pleasures of all kinds: death, with one stroke of his desolating hand, shall one day strip us bare to a winding-sheet and a coffin of all the things we are so mad to possess. But the last enemy, with all his malice and all his resistless power, cannot touch our moral character—unless it be in some way utterly mysterious to us that he is made under God to refine and perfect it. The Express Image carried up to His Father's House, not only the divine life He had brought hither with Him when He came to obey and submit and suffer among us; He carried back more than He brought, for He carried back a human heart, a human life, a human character, which was and is a new wonder in heaven. He carried up to heaven all the love to God and angels and men He had learned and practised on earth, with all the earthly fruits of it. He carried back His humility, His meekness, His humanity, His approachableness, and His sympathy. And we see to our salvation some of the uses to which those parts of His moral character are at this moment being put in His Father's House; and what we see not now of all the ends and uses and employments of our Lord's glorified humanity we shall, mayhap, see hereafter. And we also shall carry our moral character to heaven; it is the only thing we have worth carrying so far. But, then, moral character is well worth achieving here and then carrying there, for it is nothing else and nothing less than the divine nature itself; it is the divine nature incarnate, incorporate, and made manifest in man. And it is, therefore, immortal with the immortality of God, and blessed for ever with the blessedness of God.

II

EVANGELIST

'Do the work of an evangelist.'—Paul to Timothy.

N the 1st of June 1648 a very bitter fight was fought at Maidstone, in Kent, between the Parliamentary forces under Fairfax and the Royalists. Till Cromwell rose to all his military and administrative greatness, Fairfax was general-issimo of the Puritan army, and that able soldier never executed a more brilliant exploit than he did that memorable night at Maidstone. In one night the Royalist insurrection was stamped out and extinguished in its own blood. Hundreds of dead bodies filled the streets of the town, hundreds of the enemy were taken prisoners, while hundreds more, who were hiding in the hop-fields and forests around the town, fell into Fairfax's hands next morning.

Among the prisoners so taken was a Royalist major who had had a deep hand in the Maidstone insurrection, named John Gifford, a man who was destined in the time to come to run a remarkable career Only, to-day, the day after the battle, he has no prospect before him but the gallows. On the night before his execution, by the courtesy of Fairfax, Gifford's sister was permitted to visit her brother in his prison. The soldiers were overcome with weariness and sleep after the engagement, and Gifford's sister so managed it that her brother got past the sentries and escaped out of the town. He lay hid for some days in the ditches and thickets around the town till he was able to escape to London, and thence to the shelter of some friends of his at Bedford. Gifford had studied medicine before he entered the army, and as soon as he thought it safe he began to practise his old art in the town of Bedford. Gifford had been a dissolute man as a soldier, and he became, if possible, a still more scandalously dissolute man as a civilian. Gifford's life in Bedford was a public disgrace, and his hatred and persecution of the Puritans in that town made his very name an infamy and a fear. He reduced himself to beggary with gambling and drink, but, when near suicide, he came under the power of the truth, till we see him clothed with rags and with a great burden on his back, crying out, 'What must I do to be saved?' 'But at last'—I quote from the session records of his future church at Bedford—'God did so plentifully discover to him the forgiveness of sins for the sake of Christ, that all his life after he lost not the light of God's countenance, no, not for an hour, save only about two days before he died.' Gifford's conversion had been so conspicuous and notorious that both town and country soon heard of it : and instead of being ashamed of it, and seeking to hide it, Gifford at once, and openly, threw in his lot with the extremest Puritans in the Puritan town of Bedford. Nor could Gifford's talents be hid ; till from one thing to another, we find the former Royalist and dissolute Cavalier actually the parish minister of Bedford in Cromwell's so evangelical but otherwise so elastic establishment.

At this point we open John Bunyan's *Grace Abounding to the Chief of Sinners*, and we read this classical passage :—' Upon a day the good providence of God did cast me to Bedford to work in my calling : and in one of the streets of that town I came where there were three or four poor women sitting at the door in the sun and talking about the things of God. But I may say I heard, but I understood not, for they were far above and out of my reach. . . . About this time I began to break my mind to those poor people in Bedford, and to tell them of my condition, which, when they had heard, they told Mr. Gifford of me, who himself also took occasion to talk with me, and was willing to be well persuaded of me though I think on too little grounds. But he invited me to his house, where I should hear him confer with others about the dealings of God with their souls, from all which I still received more conviction, and from that time began to see something of the vanity and inner wretchedness of my own heart, for as yet I knew no great matter therein. . . . At that time also I sat under the ministry of holy Mr. Gifford, whose doctrine, by the grace of God, was much for my stability.' And so on in that inimitable narrative.

The first minister whose words were truly blessed of God for our awakening and conversion has always a place of his own in our hearts. We all have some minister, some revivalist, some faithful friend, or some good book in a warm place in our heart. It may be a great city preacher; it may be a humble American or Irish revivalist; it may be *The Pilgrim's Progress*, or *The Cardiphonia*, or the *Serious Call*— whoever or whatever it was that first arrested and awakened and turned us into the way of life, they all our days stand in a place by themselves in our grateful heart. And John Gifford has been immortalised by John Bunyan, both in his *Grace Abounding* and in his *Pilgrim's Progress*. In his *Grace Abounding*, as we have just seen, and in *The Pilgrim*, Gifford has his portrait painted in holy oil on the wall of the Interpreter's house, and again in eloquent pen and ink in the person of Evangelist.

John Gifford had himself made a narrow escape out of the City of Destruction, and John Bunyan had, by Gifford's assistance, made the same escape also. The scene, therefore, both within that city and outside the gate of it, was so fixed in Bunyan's mind and memory that no part of his memorable book is more memorably put than just its opening page. Bunyan himself is the man in rags, and Gifford is the evangelist who comes to console and to conduct him. Bunyan's portraits are all taken from the life. Brilliant and well-furnished as Bunyan's imagination was, Bedford was still better furnished with all kinds of men and women, and with all kinds of saints and sinners. And thus, instead of drawing upon his imagination in writing his books, Bunyan drew from life. And thus it is that we see first John Gifford, and then John Bunyan himself at the gate of the city; and then, over the page, Gifford becomes the evangelist who is sent by the four poor women to speak to the awakened tinker.

'Wherefore dost thou so cry?' asks Evangelist. 'Because,' replied the man, 'I am condemned to die.' 'But why are you so unwilling to die, since this life is so full of evils?' And I suppose we must all hear Evangelist putting the same pungent question to ourselves every day, at whatever point of the celestial journey we at present are. Yes; why are we all so unwilling to die? Why do we number our days to put off our death to the last possible period? Why do we so refuse to think of the only thing we are sure soon to come to? We are absolutely sure of nothing else in the future but death. We may not see to-morrow, but we shall certainly see the day of our death. And yet we have all our plans laid for to-morrow, and only one here and one there has any plan laid for the day of his death. And can it be for the same reason that made the man in rags unwilling to die? Is it because of the burden on our back? Is it because we are not fit to go to judgment? And yet the trumpet may sound summoning us hence before the midnight clock strikes. If this be thy condition, why standest thou still? Dost thou see yonder shining light? Keep that light in thine eye. Go up straight to it, knock at the gate, and it shall be told thee there what thou shalt do next. Burdened sinner, son of man in rags and terror: What has burdened thee so? What has torn thy garments into such shameful rags? What is it in thy burden that makes it so heavy? And how long has it lain so heavy upon thee? 'I cannot run,' said the man, 'because of the burden on my back.' And it has been noticed of you that you do not laugh, or run, or dress, or dance, or walk, or eat, or drink as once you did. All men see that there is some burden on your back; some sore burden on your heart and your mind. Do you see yonder wicket gate? Do you see yonder shining light? There is no light in all the horizon for you but yonder light over the gate. Keep it in your eye; make straight, and make at once for it, and He who keeps the gate and keeps the light burning over it, He will tell you what to do with your burden. He told John Gifford, and He told John Bunyan, till both their burdens rolled off their backs, and they saw them no more. What would you not give to-night to be released like them? Do you not see yonder shining light?

Having set Christian fairly on the way to the wicket gate, Evangelist leaves him in order to seek out and assist some other seeker. But yesterday he had set Faithful's face to the celestial city, and he is off now to look for another pilgrim. We know some of Christian's adventures and episodes after Evangelist left him, but we do not take up these at present. We pass on to the next time that Evangelist finds Christian, and he finds him in a sorry plight. He has listened to bad advice. He has gone off the right road, he has lost sight of the gate, and all the thunders and lightnings of Sinai are rolling and flashing out against him. What doest thou here of all men in the world? asked Evangelist, with a severe and dreadful countenance. Did I not direct thee to His gate, and why art thou here? Christian told him that a fair-spoken man had met him, and had persuaded him to take an easier and shorter

way of getting rid of his burden. Read the whole
place for yourselves. The end of it was that Evangelist set Christian right again, and gave him two
counsels which would be his salvation if he attended
to them: Strive to enter in at the strait gate, and,
Take up thy cross daily. He would need more
counsel afterwards than that; but, meantime, that
was enough. Let Christian follow that, and he
would before long be rid of his burden.

In the introductory lecture Bishop Butler has been
commended and praised as a moralist, and certainly
not one word beyond his deserts; but an evangelical
preacher cannot send any man with the burden of a
bad past upon him to Butler for advice and direction
about that. While lecturing on and praising the sound
philosophical and ethical spirit of the great bishop,
Dr. Chalmers complains that he so much lacks the
sal evangelicum, the strength and the health and the
sweetness of the doctrines of grace. Legality and
Civility and Morality are all good and necessary in
their own places; but he is a cheat who would send
a guilt-burdened and sick-at-heart sinner to any or
all of them. The wicket gate first, and then He
who keeps that gate will tell us what to do, and
where next to go; but any other way out of the
City of Destruction but by the wicket gate is sure
to land us where it landed Evangelist's quaking and
sweating charge. When Bishop Butler lay on his
deathbed he called for his chaplain, and said,
'Though I have endeavoured to avoid sin, and to
please God to the utmost of my power, yet from
the consciousness of my perpetual infirmities I am
still afraid to die.' 'My lord,' said his happily

evangelical chaplain, 'have you forgotten that Jesus Christ is a Saviour?' 'True,' said the dying philosopher, 'but how shall I know that He is a Saviour for me?' 'My lord, it is written, "Him that cometh to Me, I will in no wise cast out."' 'True,' said Butler, 'and I am surprised that though I have read that Scripture a thousand times, I never felt its virtue till this moment, and now I die in peace.'

The third and the last time on which the pilgrims meet with their old friend and helper, Evangelist, is when they are just at the gates of the town of Vanity. They have come through many wonderful experiences since last they saw and spoke with him. They have had the gate opened to them by Goodwill. They have been received and entertained in the Interpreter's House, and in the House Beautiful. The burden has fallen off their backs at the cross, and they have had their rags removed and have received change of raiment. They have climbed the Hill Difficulty, and they have fought their way through the Valley of the Shadow of Death. More than the half of their adventures and sufferings are past; but they are not yet out of gunshot of the devil, and the bones of many a promising pilgrim lie whitening the way between this and the city. Many of our young communicants have made a fair and a promising start for salvation. They have got over the initial difficulties that lay in their way to the Lord's table, and we have entered their names with honest pride in our communion roll. But a year or two passes over, and the critical season arrives when our young communicant 'comes out,' as the word is. Up till now she has been a child, a little maid, a Bible-class student, a young communicant, a Sabbath-school teacher. But she is now a young lady, and she comes out into the world. We soon see that she has so come out, as we begin to miss her from places and from employments her presence used to brighten; and, very unwillingly, we overhear men and women with her name on their lips in a way that makes us fear for her soul, till many, oh, in a single ministry, how many, who promised well at the gate and ran safely past many snares, at last sell all—body and soul and Saviour—in Vanity Fair.

Well, Evangelist remains Evangelist still. Only, without losing any of his sweetness and freeness and fulness of promise, he adds to that some solemn warnings and counsels suitable now, as never before, to these two pilgrims. If one may say so, he would add now such moral treatises as Butler's *Sermons* and Law's *Serious Call* to such evangelical books as *Grace Abounding* and *A Jerusalem Sinner Saved*.

To-morrow the two pilgrims will come out of the wilderness and will be plunged into a city where they will be offered all kinds of merchandise,—houses, lands, places, honours, preferments, titles, pleasures, delights, wives, children, bodies, souls, and what not. An altogether new world from anything they have yet come through, and a world where many who once began well have gone no further. Such counsels as these, then, Evangelist gave Christian and Faithful as they left the lonely wilderness behind them and came out towards the gate of the

seductive city—'Let the Kingdom of Heaven be
always before your eyes, and believe steadfastly
concerning things that are invisible.' Visible,
tangible, sweet, and desirable things will immediately
be offered to them, and unless they have a faith in
their hearts that is the substance of things hoped
for, and the evidence of things not seen, it will soon
be all over with them and their pilgrimage. 'Let
no man take your crown,' he said also, as he foresaw
at how many booths and counters, houses, lands,
places, preferments, wives, husbands, and what not,
would be offered them and pressed upon them in
exchange for their heavenly crown. 'Above all, look
well to your own hearts,' he said. Canon Venables
laments over the teaching that Bunyan received
from John Gifford. 'Its principle,' he says, 'was
constant introspection and scrupulous weighing of
every word and deed, and even of every thought,
instead of leading the mind off from self to the
Saviour.' The canon seems to think that it was
specially unfortunate for Bunyan to be told to keep
his heart and to weigh well every thought of it;
but I must point out to you that Evangelist puts
as above all other things the most important for the
pilgrims the looking well to their own hearts; and
our plain-spoken author has used a very severe word
about any minister who should whisper anything to
any pilgrim that could be construed or misunder-
stood into putting Christ in the place of thought
and word and deed, and the scrupulous weighing of
every one of them. 'Let nothing that is on this
side the other world get within you; and above all,

look well to your own hearts, and to the lusts thereof.'

'Set your faces like a flint,' Evangelist proceeds. How little like all that you hear in the counsels of the pulpit to young women coming out and to young men entering into business life. I am convinced that if we ministers were more direct and plain-spoken to such persons at such times; if we, like Bunyan, told them plainly what kind of a world it is they are coming out to buy and sell in, and what its merchandise and its prices are; if our people would let us so preach to their sons and daughters, I feel sure far fewer young communicants would make shipwreck, and far fewer grey heads would go down with sorrow to the grave. 'Be not afraid,' said Robert Hall in his charge to a young minister, 'of devoting whole sermons to particular parts of moral conduct and religious duty. It is impossible to give right views of them unless you dissect char-acters and describe particular virtues and vices. The works of the flesh and the fruits of the Spirit must be distinctly pointed out. To preach against sin in general without descending to particulars may lead many to complain of the evil of their hearts, while at the same time they are awfully inattentive to the evil of their conduct.' Take Evangelist's noble counsels at the gate of Vanity Fair, and then take John Bunyan's masterly description of the Fair itself, with all that is bought and sold in it, and you will have a lesson in evangelical preaching that the evangelical pulpit needed in Bunyan's day, in Robert Hall's day, and not less in our own.

‘ My sons, you have heard the truth of the gospel, that you must through many tribulations enter the Kingdom of God. When, therefore, you are come to the Fair and shall find fulfilled what I have here related, then remember your friend ; quit yourselves like men, and commit the keeping of your souls to your God in well-doing as unto a faithful Creator.’

III

OBSTINATE

'Be ye not as the mule.'—*David.*

ITTLE Obstinate was born and brought up in the City of Destruction. His father was old Spare-the-Rod, and his mother's name was Spoil-the-Child. Little Obstinate was the only child of his parents; he was born when they were no longer young, and they doted on their only child, and gave him his own way in everything. Everything he asked for he got, and if he did not immediately get it you would have heard his screams and his kicks three doors off. His parents were not in themselves bad people, but, if Solomon speaks true, they hated their child, for they gave him all his own way in everything, and nothing would ever make them say no to him, or lift up the rod when he said no to them. When the Scriptures, in their pedagogical parts, speak so often about the rod, they do not necessarily mean a rod of iron or even of wood. There are other ways of teaching an obstinate child than the way that Gideon took with the men of Succoth when he taught them with the thorns of the wilderness and with the briars thereof. George Offor, John Bunyan's somewhat quaint editor, gives the readers of his edition this personal testimony :—' After bringing up a very large family, who are a blessing to their parents, I have yet to learn what part of the human body was created to be beaten.' At the same time the rod must mean something in the word of God; it certainly means something in God's hand when His obstinate children are under it, and it ought to mean something in a godly parent's hand also. Little Obstinate's two parents were far from ungodly people, though they lived in such a city; but they were daily destroying their only son by letting him always have his own way, and by never saying no to his greed, and his lies, and his anger, and his noisy and disorderly ways. Eli in the Old Testament was not a bad man, but he destroyed both the ark of the Lord and himself and his sons also, because his sons made themselves vile, and he restrained them not. God's children are never so soft, and sweet, and good, and happy as just after He restrains them, and has again laid the rod of correction upon them. They then kiss both the rod and Him who appointed it. And earthly fathers learn their craft from God. The meekness, the sweetness, the docility, and the love of a chastised child has gone to all our hearts in a way we can never forget. There is something sometimes almost past description or belief in the way a chastised child clings to and kisses the hand that chastised it. But poor old Spare-the-Rod never had experiences like that. And young Obstinate, having been born like Job's wild ass's colt, grew up to be a man like David's unbitted and unbridled mule, till in after life he became the author of all the evil and mischief that is associated in our minds with his evil name.

In old Spare-the-Rod's child also this true proverb
was fulfilled, that the child is the father of the man.
For all that little Obstinate had been in the nursery,
in the schoolroom, and in the playground—all that,
only in an aggravated way—he was as a youth and
as a grown-up man. For one thing, Obstinate all
his days was a densely ignorant man. He had not
got into the way of learning his lessons when he was
a child; he had not been made to learn his lessons
when he was a child; and the dislike and contempt
he had for his books as a boy accompanied him
through an ignorant and a narrow-minded life. It
was reason enough to this so unreasonable man not
to buy and read a book that you had asked him to
buy and read it. And so many of the books about
him were either written, or printed, or published, or
sold, or read, or praised by people he did not like,
that there was little left for this unhappy man to
read, even if otherwise he would have read it. And
thus, as his mulish obstinacy kept him so ignorant,
so his ignorance in turn increased his obstinacy.
And then when he came, as life went on, to have
anything to do with other men's affairs, either in
public or in private life, either in the church, or in
the nation, or in the city, or in the family, this
unhappy man could only be a drag on all kinds of
progress, and an obstacle to every good work. Use
and wont, a very good rule on occasion, was a rigid
and a universal rule with Obstinate. And to be told
that the wont in this case and in that had ceased
to be the useful, only made him rail at you as only
an ignorant and an obstinate man can rail. He
could only rail; he had not knowledge enough, or

good temper enough, or good manners enough to reason out a matter; he was too hot-tempered for an argument, and he hated those who had an acquaintance with the subject in hand, and a self-command in connection with it that he had not. 'The obstinate man's understanding is like Pharaoh's heart, and it is proof against all sorts of arguments whatsoever.' Like the demented king of Egypt, the obstinate man has glimpses sometimes both of his bounden duty and of his true interest, but the sinew of iron that is in his neck will not let him perform the one or pursue the other. 'Nothing,' says a penetrating writer, 'is more like firm conviction than simple obstinacy. Plots and parties in the state, and heresies and divisions in the church alike proceed from it.' Let any honest man take that sentence and carry it like a candle down into his own heart and back into his own life, and then with the insight and honesty there learned carry the same candle back through some of the plots and parties, the heresies and schisms of the past as well as of the present day, and he will have learned a lesson that will surely help to cure himself, at any rate, of his own remaining obstinacy. All our firm convictions, as we too easily and too fondly call them, must continually be examined and searched out in the light of more reading of the best authors, in the light of more experience of ourselves and of the world we live in, and in that best of all light, that increasing purity, simplicity, and sincerity of heart alone can kindle. And in not a few instances we shall to a certainty find that what has hitherto been clothing itself with the honourable name and character of a conviction was all the time only an ignorant prejudice, a distaste or a dislike, a too great fondness for ourselves and for our own opinion and our own interest. Many of our firmest convictions, as we now call them, when we shall have let light enough fall upon them, we shall be compelled and enabled to confess to be at bottom mere mulishness and pride of heart. The mulish, obstinate, and proud man never says, I don't know. He never asks anything to be explained to him. He never admits that he has got any new light. He never admits having spoken or acted wrongly. He never takes back what he has said. He was never heard to say, You are right in that line of action, and I have all along been wrong. Had he ever said that, the day he said it would have been a white-stone day both for his mind and his heart. Only, the spoiled son of Spare-the-Rod never said that, or anything like that.

But, most unfortunately, it is in the very best things of life that the true mulishness of the obstinate man most comes out. He shows worst in his home life and in the matters of religion. When our Obstinate was in love he was as sweet as honey and as soft as butter. His old friends that he used so to trample upon scarcely recognised him. They had sometimes seen men converted, but they had never seen such an immediate and such a complete conversion as this. He actually invited correction, and reproof, and advice, and assistance, who had often struck at you with his hands and his feet when you even hinted at such a thing to him. The best upbringing, the best books, the best preaching, the best and most obedient life, taken all together, had not done for other men what a woman's smile and the touch of her hand had in a moment done for this once so obstinate man. He would read anything now, and especially the best books. He would hear and enjoy any preacher now, and especially the best and most earnest in preaching. His old likes and dislikes, prejudices and prepossessions, self-opinionativeness and self-assertiveness all miraculously melted off him, and he became in a day an open-minded, intelligent, good-mannered, devout-minded gentleman. He who was once such a mule to everybody was now led about by a child in a silken bridle. All old things had passed away, and all things had become new. For a time; for a time. But time passes, and there passes away with it all the humility, meekness, pliability, softness, and sweetness of the obstinate man. Till when long enough time has elapsed you find him all the obstinate and mulish man he ever was. It is not that he has ceased to love his wife and his children. It is not that. But there is this in all genuine and inbred obstinacy, that after a time it often comes out worst beside those we love best. A man will be affable, accessible, entertaining, the best of company, and the soul of it abroad, and, then, instantly he turns the latch-key in his own door he will relapse into silence, and sink back into utter boorishness and bearishness, mulishness and doggedness. He swallows his evening meal at the foot of the table in silence, and then he sits all night at the fireside with a cloud out of nothing on his brow. His sunshine, his smile, and his universal urbanity is all gone now; he is discourteous to nobody but to his own wife. Nothing pleases him; he finds nothing at home to his mind. The furniture, the hours, the habits of the house are all disposed so as to please him; but he was never yet heard to say to wife, or child, or servant that he was pleased. He never says that a meal is to his taste or a seat set so as to shelter and repose him. The obstinate man makes his house a very prison and treadmill to himself and to all those who are condemned to suffer with him. And all the time it is not that he does not love and honour his household; but by an evil law of the obstinate heart its worst obstinacy and mulishness comes out among those it loves best.

But, my brethren, worse than all that, we have all what good Bishop Hall calls ' a stone of obstination' in our hearts against God. With all his own depth and clearness and plain-spokenness, Paul tells us that our hearts are by nature enmity against God. Were we proud and obstinate and malicious against men only it would be bad enough, and it would be difficult enough to cure, but our case is dreadful beyond all description or belief when our obstinacy strikes out against God. We know as well as we know anything, that in doing this and in not doing that we are going every day right in the teeth both of God's law and God's grace; and yet in the sheer obstinacy and perversity of our heart we still go on in what we know quite well to be the suicide of our souls. We are told by our minister to do this and not to do that; to begin to do this at this new year and to break off from doing that;

but, partly through obstinacy towards him, reinforced by a deeper and subtler and deadlier obstinacy against God, and against all the deepest and most godly of the things of God, we neither do the one nor cease from doing the other. There is a sullenness in some men's minds, a gloom and a bitter air that rises up from the unploughed, undrained, unweeded, uncultivated fens of their hearts that chills and blasts all the feeble beginnings of a better life. The natural and constitutional obstinacy of the obstinate heart is exasperated when it comes to deal with the things of God. For it is then reinforced with all the guilt and all the fear, all the suspicion and all the aversion of the corrupt and self-condemned heart. There is an obdurateness of obstinacy against all the men, and the books, and the doctrines, and the precepts, and the practices that are in any way connected with spiritual religion that does not come out even in the obstinate man's family life.

John Bunyan's Obstinate, both by his conduct as well as by the etymology of his name, not only stands in the way of his own salvation, but he does all he can to stand in the way of other men setting out to salvation also. Obstinate set out after Christian to fetch him back by force, and if it had not been that he met his match in Christian, *The Pilgrim's Progress* would never have been written. 'That can by no means be,' said Christian to his pursuer, and he is first called Christian when he shows that one man can be as obstinate in good as another man can be in evil. 'I never now can go back to my former life.' And then the two ob-

stinate men parted company for ever, Christian in
holy obstinacy being determined to have eternal
life at any cost, and Obstinate as determined against
it. The opening pages of the *The Pilgrim's Progress*
set the two men very graphically and very impres-
sively before us.

As to the cure of obstinacy, the rod in a firm,
watchful, wise, and loving hand will cure it. And
in later life a long enough and close enough suc-
cession of humble, yielding, docile, submissive, self-
chastening and thanksgiving acts will cure it.
Reading and obeying the best books on the subjugation and the regulation of the heart will cure
it. Descending with Dante to where the obstinate,
and the embittered, and the gloomy, and the sullen
have made their beds in hell will cure it. And
much and most agonising prayer will above all
cure it.

> ' O Lord, if thus so obstinate I,
>   Choose Thou, before my spirit die,
>   A piercing pain, a killing sin,
>   And to my proud heart run them in.

IV

PLIABLE

'He hath not root in himself.'—*Our Lord*.

WITH one stroke of His pencil our Lord gives us this Flaxman-like outline of one of his well-known hearers. And then John Bunyan takes up that so expressive profile, and puts flesh and blood into it, till it becomes the well-known Pliable of *The Pilgrim's Progress*. We call the text a parable, but our Lord's parables are all portraits— portraits and groups of portraits, rather than ordinary parables. Our Lord knew this man quite well who had no root in himself. Our Lord had crowds of such men always running after Him, and He threw off this rapid portrait from hundreds of men and women who caused discredit to fall on His name and His work, and burdened His heart continually. And John Bunyan, with all his genius, could never have given us such speaking likenesses as that of Pliable and Temporary and Talkative, unless he had had scores of them in his own congregation.

Our Lord's short preliminary description of Pliable goes, like all His descriptions, to the very bottom of the whole matter. Our Lord in this passage is like one of those masterly artists who begin their

portrait-painting with the study of anatomy. All
the great artists in this walk build up their best
portraits from the inside of their subjects. He hath
not root in himself, says our Lord, and we need no
more than that to be told us to foresee how all his
outside religion will end. 'Without self-knowledge,'
says one of the greatest students of the human
heart that ever lived, 'you have no real root in
yourselves. Real self-knowledge is the root of all
real religious knowledge. It is a deceit and a
mischief to think that the Christian doctrines can
either be understood or aright accepted by any
outward means. It is just in proportion as we
search our own hearts and understand our own
nature that we shall ever feel what a blessing the
removal of sin will be; redemption, pardon, sancti-
cation, are all otherwise mere words without meaning or power to us. God speaks to us first in our
own hearts.' Happily for us our Lord has annotated
His own text and has told us that an honest heart
is the alone root of all true religion. Honest, that
is, with itself, and with God and man about itself.
As David says in his so honest psalm, 'Behold, Thou
desirest truth in the inward parts, and in the
hidden part Thou shalt make me to know wisdom.'
And, indeed, all the preachers and writers in Scripture, and all Scriptural preachers and writers outside
of Scripture, are at one in this: that all true wisdom
begins at home, and that it all begins at the heart.
And they all teach us that he is the wisest of men
who has the worst opinion of his own heart, as he
is the foolishest of men who does not know his own
heart to be the worst heart that ever any man was

cursed with in this world. 'Here is wisdom': not to know the number of the beast, but to know his mark, and to read it written so indelibly in our own heart.

And where this first and best of all wisdom is not, there, in our Lord's words, there is no deepness of earth, no root, and no fruit. And any religion that most men have is of this outside, shallow, rootless description. This was all the religion that poor Pliable ever had. This poor creature had a certain slight root of something that looked like religion for a short season, but even that slight root was all outside of himself. His root, what he had of a root, was all in Christian's companionship and impassioned appeals, and then in those impressive passages of Scripture that Christian read to him. At your first attention to these things you would think that no possible root could be better planted than in the Bible and in earnest preaching. But even the Bible, and, much more, the best preaching, is all really outside of a man till true religion once gets its piercing roots down into himself. We have perhaps all heard of men, and men of no small eminence, who were brought up to believe the teaching of the Bible and the pulpit, but who, when some of their inherited and external ideas about some things connected with the Bible began to be shaken, straightway felt as if all the grounds of their faith were shaken, and all the roots of their faith pulled up. But where that happened, all that was because such men's religion was all rooted outside of themselves; in the best things outside of themselves, indeed, but because, in our

Lord's words, their religion was rooted in something outside of themselves and not inside, they were by and by offended, and threw off their faith. There is another well-known class of men all whose religion is rooted in their church, and in their church not as a member of the body of Christ, but as a social institution set up in this world. They believe in their church. They worship their church. They suffer and make sacrifices for their church. They are proud of the size and the income of their church; her past contendings and sufferings, and present dangers, all endear their church to their heart. But if tribulation and persecution arise, that is to say, if anything arises to vex or thwart or disappoint them with their church, they incontinently pull up their roots and their religion with it, and transplant both to any other church that for the time better pleases them, or to no church at all. Others, again, have all their religiosity rooted in their family life. Their religion is all made up of domestic sentiment. They love their earthly home with that supreme satisfaction and that all-absorbing affection that truly religious men entertain for their heavenly home. And thus it is that when anything happens to disturb or break up their earthly home their rootless religiosity goes with it. Other men's religion, again, and all their interest in it, is rooted in their shop; you can make them anything or nothing in religion, according as you do or do not do business in their shop. Companionship, also, accounts for the fluctuations of many men's, and almost all women's, religious lives. If they happen to fall in with godly lovers and friends, they are

sincerely godly with them; but if their companions
are indifferent or hostile to true religion, they
gradually fall into the same temper and attitude.
We sometimes see students destined for the Christian ministry also with all their religion so without
root in themselves that a session in an unsympathetic
class, a sceptical book, sometimes just a sneer or a
scoff, will wither all the promise of their coming
service. And so on through the whole of human
life. He that hath not the root of the matter in
himself dureth for a while, but by and by,
for one reason or another, he is sure to be
offended.

So much, then,—not enough, nor good enough—for
our Lord's swift stroke at the heart of His hearers.
But let us now pass on to Pliable, as he so soon and
so completely discovers himself to us under John
Bunyan's so skilful hand. Look well at our author's
speaking portrait of a well-known man in Bedford
who had no root in himself, and who, as a consequence, was pliable to any influence, good or bad,
that happened to come across him. 'Don't revile,'
are the first words that come from Pliable's lips,
and they are not unpromising words. Pliable is
hurt with Obstinate's coarse abuse of the Christian
life, till he is downright ashamed to be seen in his
company. Pliable, at least, is a gentleman compared with Obstinate, and his gentlemanly feelings
and his good manners make him at once take sides
with Christian. Obstinate's foul tongue has almost
made Pliable a Christian. And this finely-conceived
scene on the plain outside the city gate is enacted
over again every day among ourselves. Where men

are in dead earnest about religion it always arouses the bad passions of bad men; and where earnest preachers and devoted workers are assailed with violence or with bad language, there is always enough love of fair play in the bystanders to compel them to take sides, for the time at least, with those who suffer for the truth. And we are sometimes too apt to count all that love of common fairness, and that hatred of foul play, as a sure sign of some sympathy with the hated truth itself. When an onlooker says 'Don't revile,' we are too ready to set down that expression of civility as at least the first beginning of true religion. But the religion of Jesus Christ cuts far deeper into the heart of man than to the dividing asunder of justice and injustice, civility and incivility, ribaldry and good manners. And it is always found in the long-run that the cross of Christ and its crucifixion of the human heart goes quite as hard with the gentlemanly-mannered man, the civil and urbane man, as it does with the man of bad behaviour and of brutish manners. 'Civil men,' says Thomas Goodwin, 'are this world's saints.' And poor Pliable was one of them. 'My heart really inclines to go with my neighbour,' said Pliable next. 'Yes,' he said, 'I begin to come to a point. I really think I will go along with this good man. Yes, I will cast in my lot with him. Come, good neighbour, let us be going.'

The apocalyptic side of some men's imaginations is very easily worked upon. No kind of book sells better among those of our people who have no root in themselves than just picture-books about heaven.

Our missionaries make use of lantern-slides to bring home the scenes in the Gospels to the dull minds of their village hearers, and with good success. And at home a magic-lantern filled with the splendours of the New Jerusalem would carry multitudes of rootless hearts quite captive for a time. 'Well said; and what else? This is excellent; and what else?' Christian could not tell Pliable fast enough about the glories of heaven. 'There we shall be with seraphim and cherubim, creatures that will dazzle your eyes to look on them. There also you shall meet with thousands and ten thousands who have gone before us to that place. Elders with golden crowns, and holy virgins with golden harps, and all clothed with immortality as with a garment.' 'The hearing of all this,' cried Pliable, 'is enough to ravish one's heart.' 'An overly faith,' says old Thomas Shepard, 'is easily wrought.'

As if the text itself was not graphic enough, Bunyan's racy, humorous, pathetic style overflows the text and enriches the very margins of his pages, as every possessor of a good edition of *The Pilgrim* knows. 'Christian and Obstinate pull for Pliable's soul' is the eloquent summary set down on the side of the sufficiently eloquent page. As the picture of a man's soul being pulled for rises before my mind, I can think of no better companion picture to that of Pliable than that of poor, hard-beset Brodie of Brodie, as he lets us see the pull for his soul in the honest pages of his inward diary. Under the head of 'Pliable' in my Bunyan note-book I find a crowd of references to Brodie; and if only to illustrate our author's marginal note, I shall transcribe one or two of them. 'The writer of this diary desires to be cast down under the facileness and plausibleness of his nature, by which he labours to please men more than God, and whence it comes that the wicked speak good of him. . . . The Lord pity the proneness of his heart to comply with the men who have the power. . . . Lord, he is unsound and double in his heart, politically crafty, selfish, not savouring nor discerning the things of God. . . . Let not self-love, wit, craft, and timorousness corrupt his mind, but indue him with fortitude, patience, steadfastness, tenderness, mortification. . . . Shall I expose myself and my family to danger at this time ? A grain of sound faith would solve all my questions.' 'Die Dom. I stayed at home, partly to decline the ill-will and rage of men and to decline observation.' Or, take another Sabbath-day entry : 'Die Dom. I stayed at home, because of the time, and the observation, and the Earl of Moray. . . . Came to Cuttiehillock. I am neither cold nor hot. I am not rightly principled as to the time. I suspect that it is not all conscience that makes me conform, but wit, and to avoid suffering ; Lord, deliver me from all this unsoundness of heart.' And after this miserable fashion do heaven and earth, duty and self-interest, the covenant and the crown pull for Lord Brodie's soul through 422 quarto pages. Brodie's diary is one of the most humiliating, heart-searching, and heart-instructing books I ever read. Let all public men tempted and afflicted with a facile, pliable, time-serving heart have honest Brodie at their elbow.

'Glad I am, my good companion,' said Pliable,

after the passage about the cherubim and the seraphim, and the golden crowns and the golden harps,
'it ravishes my very heart to hear all this. Come
on, let us mend our pace.' This is delightful, this
is perfect. How often have we ourselves heard
these very words of challenge and reproof from the
pliable frequenters of emotional meetings, and from
the emotional members of an emotional but rootless
ministry. Come on, let us mend our pace! 'I am
sorry to say,' replied the man with the burden on
his back, 'that I cannot go so fast as I would.'
'Christian,' says Mr. Kerr Bain, 'has more to carry
than Pliable has, as, indeed, he would still have if
he were carrying nothing but himself; and he does
have about him, besides, a few sobering thoughts as
to the length and labour and some of the unfore-
seen chances of the way.' And as Dean Paget says
in his profound and powerful sermon on 'The
Disasters of Shallowness' : 'Yes, but there is something else first ; something else without which that
inexpensive brightness, that easy hopefulness, is apt
to be a frail resourceless growth, withering away
when the sun is up and the hot winds of trial are
sweeping over it. We must open our hearts to our
religion ; we must have the inward soil broken up,
freely and deeply its roots must penetrate our inner
being. We must take to ourselves in silence and
in sincerity its words of judgment with its words of
hope, its sternness with its encouragement, its
denunciations with its promises, its requirements
with its offers, its absolute intolerance of sin with
its inconceivable and divine long-suffering towards
sinners.' But preaching like this would have

frightened away poor Pliable. He would not have understood it, and what he did understand of it he would have hated with all his shallow heart.

'Where are we now?' called Pliable to his companion, as they both went over head and ears into the Slough of Despond. 'Truly,' said Christian, 'I do not know.'—No work of man is perfect, not even the all-but-perfect *Pilgrim's Progress*. Christian was bound· to fall sooner or later into a slough filled with his own despondency about himself, his past guilt, his present sinfulness, and his anxious future. But Pliable had not knowledge enough of himself to make him ever despond. He was always ready and able to mend his pace. He had no burden on his back, and therefore no doubt in his heart. But Christian had enough of both for any ten men, and it was Christian's overflowing despondency and doubt at this point of the road that suddenly filled his own slough, and, I suppose, overflowed into a slough for Pliable also. Had Pliable only had a genuine and original slough of his own to so sink and be be daubed in, he would have got out of it at the right side of it, and been a tender-stepping pilgrim all his days.—'Is this the happiness you have told me all this while of? May I get out of this with my life, you may possess the brave country alone for me.' And with that he gave a desperate struggle or two, and got out of the mire on that side of the slough which was next his own house; so he went away, and Christian saw him no more. 'The side of the slough which was next his own house.' Let us close with that. Let us go home thinking about that. And in this trial of faith and patience, and in that, in this temptation to sin, and in that, in this actual transgression, and in that, let us always ask ourselves which is the side of the slough that is farthest away from our own house, and let us still struggle to that side of the slough, and it will all be well with us at the last.

V

HELP

'I was brought low, and He helped me.'—*David*.

HE Slough of Despond is one of John Bunyan's masterpieces. In his description of the slough, Bunyan touches his highest water-mark for humour, and pathos, and power, and beauty of language. If we did not have the English Bible in our own hands we would have to ask, as Lord Jeffrey asked Lord Macaulay, where the brazier of Bedford got his inimitable style. Bunyan confesses to us that he got all his Latin from the prescription papers of his doctors, and we know that he got all his perfect English from his English Bible. And then he got his humour and his pathos out of his own deep and tender heart. The God of all grace gave a great gift to the English-speaking world and to the Church of Christ in all lands when He created and converted John Bunyan, and put it into his head and his heart to compose *The Pilgrim's Progress*. His heart-affecting page on the slough has been wetted with the tears of thousands of its readers, and their tears have been mingled with smiles as they read their own sin and misery, and the never-to-be-forgotten time and place where their sin and misery first found them out, all told so recognisably, so pathetically, and so amusingly almost to laughableness in the passage upon the slough. We see the ocean of scum and filth pouring down into the slough through the subterranean sewers of the City of Destruction and of the Town of Stupidity, which lies four degrees beyond the City of Destruction, and from many other of the houses and haunts of men. We see His Majesty's sappers and miners at their wits' end how to cope with the deluges of pollution that pour into this slough that they have been ordained to drain and dry up. For ages and ages the royal surveyors have been laying out all their skill on this slough. More cartloads than you could count of the best material for filling up a slough have been shot into it, and yet you would never know that so much as a single labourer had emptied his barrow here. True, excellent stepping-stones have been laid across the slough by skilful engineers, but they are always so slippery with the scum and slime of the slough, that it is only now and then that a traveller can keep his feet upon them. Altogether, our author's picture of the Slough of Despond is such a picture that no one who has seen it can ever forget it. But better than reading the best description of the slough is to see certain well-known pilgrims trying to cross it. Mr. Fearing at the Slough of Despond was a tale often told at the tavern suppers of that country. Never pilgrim attempted the perilous journey with such a chicken-heart in his bosom as this Mr. Fearing. He lay above a month on the bank of the slough, and would not even attempt the steps. Some kind pilgrims, though they had enough to do to keep the steps themselves, offered him a hand ; but no. And after they were safely over it made them almost weep to hear the man still roaring in his horror at the other side. Some bade him go home if he would not take the steps, but he said that he would rather make his grave in the slough than go back one hairsbreadth. Till, one sunshiny morning,—no one knew how, and he never knew how himself— the steps were so high and dry, and the scum and slime were so low, that this hare-hearted man made a venture, and so got over. But, then, as an unkind friend of his said, this pitiful pilgrim had a slough of despond in his own mind which he carried always and everywhere about with him, and made him the proverb of despondency that he was and is. Only, that sunshiny morning he got over both the slough inside of him and outside of him, and was heard by Help and his family singing this song on the hither side of the slough : ' He brought me up also out of an horrible pit, out of the miry clay, and set my feet upon a rock, and established my goings.'

Our pilgrim did not have such a good crossing as Mr. Fearing. Whether it was that the discharge from the city was deeper and fouler, or that the day was darker, or what, we are not told, but both Christian and Pliable were in a moment out of sight in the slough. They both wallowed, says their plain-spoken historian, in the slough, only the one of the two who had the burden on his back at every wallow went deeper into the mire ; when his neighbour, who had no such burden, instead of coming to his assistance, got out of the slough at the same side as he had entered it, and made with all his might for his own house. But the man called

Christian made what way he could, and still tumbled on to the side of the slough that was farthest from his own house, till a man called Help gave him his hand and set him upon sound ground. Christiana, again, and Mercy and the boys found the slough in a far worse condition than it had ever been found before. And the reason was not that the country that drained into the slough was worse, but that those who had the mending of the slough and the keeping in repair of the steps had so bungled their work that they had marred the way instead of mending it. At the same time, by the tact and good sense of Mercy, the whole party got over, Mercy remarking to the mother of the boys, that if she had as good ground to hope for a loving reception at the gate as Christiana had, no slough of despond would discourage her, she said. To which the older woman made the characteristic reply: 'You know your sore and I know mine, and we shall both have enough evil to face before we come to our journey's end.'

Now, I do not for a moment suppose that there is any one here who can need to be told what the Slough of Despond in reality is. Indeed, its very name sufficiently declares it. But if any one should still be at a loss to understand this terrible experience of all the pilgrims, the explanation offered by the good man who gave Christian his hand may here be repeated. 'This miry slough,' he said, 'is such a place as cannot be mended. This slough is the descent whither the scum and filth that attends conviction of sin doth continually run, and therefore it is called by the name of Despond, for still as the sinner is awakened about his lost condition there ariseth in his soul many fears and doubts and discouraging apprehensions, which all of them get together, and settle in this place, and this is the reason of the badness of the ground.' That is the parable, with its interpretation ; but there is a passage in *Grace Abounding* which is no parable, and which may even better than this so pictorial slough describe some men's condition here. 'My original and inward pollution,' says Bunyan himself in his autobiography, 'that, that was my plague and my affliction ; that, I say, at a dreadful rate was always putting itself forth within me ; that I had the guilt of to amazement ; by reason of that I was more loathsome in my own eyes than a toad ; and I thought I was so in God's eyes also. Sin and corruption would bubble up out of my heart as naturally as water bubbles up out of a fountain. I thought now that every one had a better heart than I had. I could have changed heart with anybody. I thought none but the devil himself could equalise me for inward wickedness and pollution of mind. I fell, therefore, at the sight of my own vileness, deeply into despair, for I concluded that this condition in which I was in could not stand with a life of grace. Sure, thought I, I am forsaken of God ; sure I am given up to the devil, and to a reprobate mind.'

'Let no man, then, count me a fable maker,
Nor make my name and credit a partaker
Of their derision : what is here in view,
Of mine own knowledge I dare say is true.'

Sometimes, as with Christian at the slough, a man's way in life is all slashed up into sudden ditches and pitfalls out of the sins of his youth. His sins, by God's grace, find him out, and under their arrest and overthrow he begins to seek his way to a better life and a better world; and then both the burden and the slough have their explanation and ful-filment in his own life every day. But it is even more dreadful than a slough in a man's way to have a slough in his mind, as both Bunyan himself and Mr. Fearing, his exquisite creation, had. After the awful-enough slough, filled with the guilt and fear of actual sin, had been bridged and crossed and left behind, a still worse slough of inward corrup-tion and pollution rose up in John Bunyan's soul and threatened to engulf him altogether. So terrible to Bunyan was this experience, that he has not thought it possible to make a parable of it, and so put it into the *Pilgrim*; he has kept it rather for the plain, direct, unpictured, personal testimony of the *Grace Abounding*. I do not know another pas-sage anywhere to compare with the eighty-fourth paragraph of *Grace Abounding* for hope and encour-agement to a great inward sinner under a great inward sanctification. I commend that powerful passage to the appropriation of any man here who may have stuck fast in the Slough of Despond to-day, and who could not on that account come to the Lord's Table. Let him still struggle out at the side of the slough farthest from his own house, and to-night, who can tell, Help may come and give that man his hand. When the Slough of Despond is drained, and its bottom laid bare, what a find of all kinds of precious treasures shall be laid bare! Will you be able to lay claim to any of it when the long-lost treasure-trove is distributed by command of the King to its rightful owners?

'What are you doing there?' the man whose name was Help demanded of Christian, as he still wallowed and plunged to the hither side of the slough, 'and why did you not look for the steps?' And so saying he set Christian's feet upon sound ground again, and showed him the nearest way to the gate. Help is one of the King's officers who are planted all along the way to the Celestial City, in order to assist and counsel all pilgrims. Evangelist was one of those officers; this Help is another; Goodwill will be another, unless, indeed, he is more than a mere officer; Interpreter will be another, and Greatheart, and so on. All these are preachers and pastors and evangelists who correspond to all those names and all their offices. Only some unhappy preachers are better at pushing poor pilgrims into the slough, and pushing them down to the bottom of it, than they are at helping a sinking pilgrim out; while some other more happy preachers and pastors have their manses built at the hither side of the slough and do nothing else all their days but help pilgrims out of their slough and direct them to the gate. And then there are multitudes of so-called ministers who eat the King's bread who can neither push a proud sinner into the slough nor help a prostrate sinner out of it; no, nor point him the way when he has himself wallowed out. And then, there are men called ministers, too, who also eat the King's bread, whose voice you never hear in connection with such matters, unless it be to revile both the pilgrims and their helpers, and all who run with fear and trembling up the heavenly road. But our pilgrim was happy enough to meet with a minister to whom he could look back all his remaining pilgrimage and say: 'He brought me up also out of an horrible pit, out of the miry clay, and set my feet upon a rock, and established my goings. And he hath put a new song in my mouth, even praise to our God.'

Now, as might have been expected, there is a great deal said about all kinds of help in the Bible. After the help of God, of which the Bible and especially the more experimental Psalms are full, this fine name is then applied to many Scriptural persons, and on many Scriptural occasions. The first woman whom God Almighty made bore from her Maker to her husband this noble name. Her Father, so to speak, gave her away under this noble name. And of all the sweet and noble names that a woman bears, there is none so rich, so sweet, so lasting, and so fruitful as just her first Divine name of a helpmeet. And how favoured of God is that man to be accounted whose life still continues to draw meet help out of his wife's fulness of help, till all her and his days together he is able to say, I have of God a helpmeet indeed! For in how many sloughs do many men lie till this daughter of Help gives them her hand, and out of how many more sloughs are they all their days by her delivered and kept! Sweet, maidenly, and most sensible Mercy was a great help to widow Christiana at the slough, and to her and her sons all the way up to the river —a very present help in many a need to her future mother-in-law and her pilgrim sons. Let every young man seek his future wife of God, and let him seek her of her Divine Father under that fine, homely, divine name. For God, who knoweth what we have need of before we ask Him, likes nothing better than to make a helpmeet for those who so ask Him, and still to bring the woman to the man under that so spouse-like name.

> ' What next I bring shall please thee, be assured,
> Thy likeness, thy fit help, thy other self,
> Thy wish exactly to thy heart's desire.'

And then when the apostle is making an enumeration of the various offices and agencies in the New Testament church of his day, after apostles and teachers and gifts of healing, he says, ' helps,'— assistants, that is, succourers, especially of the sick and the aged and the poor. And we do not read that either election or ordination was needed to make any given member of the apostolic church a helper. But we do read of helpers being found by the apostle among all classes and conditions of that rich and living church ; both sexes, all ages, and all descriptions of church members bore this fine apostolic name. ' Salute Urbane, our helper in Christ. . . . Greet Priscilla and Aquila, my helpers in Christ.' And both Paul and John and all the apostles were forward to confess in their epistles how much they owed of their apostolic success, as well as of their personal comfort and joy, to the helpers, both men and women, their Lord had blessed them with.

Now, the most part of us here to-night have been

at the Lord's Table to-day. We kept our feet firm on the steps as we skirted or crossed the slough that self-examination always fills and defiles for us before every new communion. And before our Lord let us rise from His Table this morning He again said to us : 'Ye call Me Master and Lord, and ye say well, for so I am. If I then have given you My hand, and have helped you, ye ought also to help one another.' Who, then, any more will withhold such help as it is in his power to give to a sinking brother? And you do not need to go far afield seeking the slough of desponding, despairing, drowning men. This whole world is full of such sloughs. There is scarce sound ground enough in this world on which to build a slough-watcher's tower. And after it is built, the very tower itself is soon stained and blinded with the scudding slime. Where are your eyes, and full of what? Do you not see sloughs full of sinking men at your very door; ay, and inside of your best built and best kept house? Your very next neighbour; nay, your own flesh and blood, if they have nothing else of Greatheart's most troublesome pilgrim about them, have at least this, that they carry about a slough with them in their own mind and in their own heart. Have you only henceforth a heart and a hand to help, and see if hundreds of sinking hearts do not cry out your name, and hundreds of slimy hands grasp at your stretched-out arm. Sloughs of all kinds of vice, open and secret; sloughs of poverty, sloughs of youthful ignorance, temptation, and transgression; sloughs of inward gloom, family disquiet and dispute ; lonely grief; all manner of sloughs, deep and miry, where no man would suspect them. And how good, how like Christ Himself, and how well-pleasing to Him to lay down steps for such sliding feet, and to lift out another and another human soul upon sound and solid ground. 'Know ye what I have done to you? For I have given you an example, that ye should do as I have done to you. If ye know these things, happy are ye if ye do them.'

VI

MR. WORLDLY-WISEMAN

Wise in this world.'—*Paul.*

R. WORLDLY-WISEMAN has a long history behind him on which we cannot now enter at any length. As a child, the little worldling, it was observed, took much after his secular father, but much more after his scheming mother. He was already a self-seeking, self-satisfied youth ; and when he became a man and began business for himself, no man's business flourished like his. 'Nothing of news,' says his biographer in another place, 'nothing of doctrine, nothing of alteration or talk of alteration could at any time be set on foot in the town but be sure Mr. Worldly-Wiseman would be at the head or tail of it. But, to be sure, he would always decline those he deemed to be the weakest, and stood always with those, in his way of thinking, that he supposed were the strongest side.' He was a man, it was often remarked, of but one book also. Sunday and Saturday he was to be found deep in *The Architect of Fortune ; or, Advancement in Life,* a book written by its author so as to 'come home to all men's business and bosoms.' He drove over scrupulously once a Sunday to the State church, of which he was one of the most determined pillars.

He had set his mind on being Lord Mayor of the
town before long, and he was determined that his
eldest son should be called Sir Worldly-Wiseman
after him, and he chose his church accordingly.
Another of his biographers in this connection wrote
of him thus: ' Our Lord Mayor parted his religion
betwixt his conscience and his purse, and he went
to church not to serve God, but to please the king.
The face of the law made him wear the mask of the
Gospel, which he used not as a means to save his
soul, but his charges.' Such, in a short word, was
this ' sottish man' who crossed over the field to
meet with our pilgrim when he was walking solitary
by himself after his escape from the slough.

' How now, good fellow? Whither away after
this burdened manner?' What a contrast those
two men were to one another in the midst of that
plain that day! Our pilgrim was full of the most
laborious going; sighs and groans rose out of his
heart at every step; and then his burden on his
back, and his filthy, slimy rags all made him a
picture such that it was to any man's credit and
praise that he should stop to speak to him. And
then, when our pilgrim looked up, he saw a gentleman standing beside him to whom he was ashamed
to speak. For the gentleman had no burden on his
back, and he did not go over the plain laboriously.
There was not a spot or a speck, a rent or a wrinkle
on all his fine raiment. He could not have been
better appointed if he had just stepped out of the
gate at the head of the way; they can wear no
cleaner garments than his in the Celestial City
itself. ' How now, good fellow? Whither away

after this burdened manner?' 'A burdened manner, indeed, as ever I think poor creature had. And
whereas you ask me whither away, I tell you, sir, I
am going to yonder wicket gate before me; for
there, as I am informed, I shall be put into a way
to be rid of my heavy burden.' 'Hast thou a wife
and children?' Yes; he is ashamed to say that he
has. But he confesses that he cannot to-day take
the pleasure in them that he used to do Since his
sin so came upon him, he is sometimes as if he had
neither wife nor child nor a house over his head.
John Bunyan was of Samuel Rutherford's terrible
experience,—that our sins and our sinfulness poison
all our best enjoyments. We do not hear much of
Rutherford's wife and children, and that, no doubt,
for the sufficient reason that he gives us in his so
open-minded letter. But Bunyan laments over his
blind child with a lament worthy to stand beside the
lament of David over Absalom, and again over Saul
and Jonathan at Mount Gilboa. At the same time,
John Bunyan often felt sore and sad at heart that
he could not love and give all his heart to his wife
and children as they deserved to be loved and to
have all his heart. He often felt guilty as he looked
on them and knew in himself that they did not
have in him such a father as, God knew, he wished
he was, or ever in this world could hope to be.
'Yes,' he said, 'but I cannot take the pleasure in
them that I would. I am sometimes as if I had
none. My sin sometimes drives me like a man
bereft of his reason and clean demented.' 'Who
bid thee go this way to be rid of thy burden? I
beshrew him for his counsel. There is not a more

troublesome and dangerous way in the world than this is to which he hath directed thee. And besides, though I used to have some of the same burden when I was young, not since I settled in that town,' pointing to the town of Carnal-Policy over the plain, ' have I been at any time troubled in that way.' And then he went on to describe and denounce the way to the Celestial City, and he did it like a man who had been all over it, and had come back again. His alarming description of the upward way reads to us like a page out of Job, or Jeremiah, or David, or Paul. ' Hear me,' he says, ' for I am older than thou. Thou art like to meet with in the way which thou goest wearisomeness, painfulness, hunger, perils, nakedness, sword, lions, dragons, darkness, and in a word, death, and what not.' You would think that you were reading the eighth of the Romans at the thirty-fifth verse; only Mr. Worldly-Wiseman does not go on to finish the chapter. He does not go on to add, ' I am persuaded that neither death, nor life, nor angels, nor principalities, nor powers, nor things present, nor things to come, nor height, nor depth, nor any other creature, shall be able to separate us from the love of God, which is in Jesus Christ our Lord.' No; Worldly-Wiseman never reads the Romans, and he never hears a sermon on that chapter when he goes to church.

Mr. Worldly-Wiseman became positively eloquent and impressive and all but convincing as he went so graphically and cumulatively over all the sorrows that attended on the way to which this pilgrim was now setting his face. But, staggering as it all was, the man in rags and slime only smiled a sad and sobbing smile in answer, and said : 'Why, sir, this burden upon my back is far more terrible to me than all the things which you have mentioned; nay, methinks I care not what I meet with in the way, so be I can also meet with deliverance from my burden.' This is what our Lord calls a pilgrim having the root of the matter in himself. This poor soul had by this time so much wearisomeness, painfulness, hunger, perils, nakedness, sword, lions, dragons, darkness, death, and what not in himself, that all these threatened things outside of himself were but so many bugbears and hobgoblins wherewith to terrify children; they were but things to be laughed at by every man who is in earnest in the way. 'I care not what else I meet with if only I also meet with deliverance.' There speaks the true pilgrim. There speaks the man who drew down the Son of God to the cross for that man's deliverance. There speaks the man, who, mire, and rags, and burdens and all, will yet be found in the heaven of heavens where the chief of sinners shall see their Deliverer face to face, and shall at last and for ever be like Him. Peter examined Dante in heaven on faith, James examined him on hope, and John took him through his catechism on love, and the seer came out of the tent with a laurel crown on his brow. I do not know who the examiner on sin will be, but, speaking for myself on this matter, I would rather take my degree in that subject than in all the other subjects set for a sinner's examination on earth or in heaven. For to know myself, and especially, as the wise man says, to know the plague of my own heart, is the true and the only key to all other true knowledge : God and man ; the Redeemer and the devil ; heaven and hell ; faith, hope, and charity ; unbelief, despair, and malignity, and all things of that kind else, all knowledge will come to that man who knows himself, and to that man alone, and to that man in the exact measure in which he does really know himself. Listen again to this slough-stained, sin-burdened, sighing and sobbing pilgrim, who, in spite of all these things—nay, in virtue of all these things—is as sure of heaven and of the far end of heaven as if he were already enthroned there. 'Wearisomeness,' he protests, 'painfulness, hunger, perils, nakedness, sword, lions, dragons, darkness, death, and what not—why, sir, this burden on my back is far more terrible to me than all these things which you have mentioned ; nay, methinks I care not what I meet with in the way, so be I can also meet with deliverance from my burden.' O God ! let this same mind be found in me and in all the men and women for whose souls I shall have to answer at the day of judgment, and I shall be content and safe before Thee.

That strong outburst from this so forfoughten man for a moment quite overawed Worldly-Wiseman. He could not reply to an earnestness like this. He did not understand it, and could not account for it. The only thing he ever was in such earnestness as that about was his success in business and his title that he and his wife were scheming for. But still, though silenced by this unaccountable outburst of our pilgrim, Worldly-Wiseman's enmity against the upward way, and especially against all the men and all the books that made pilgrims take to that way, was not silenced. 'How camest thou by thy burden at first?' 'By reading this Book in my hand.' Worldly-Wiseman did not fall foul of the Book indeed, but he fell all the more foul of those who meddled with matters they had not a head for. 'Leave these high and deep things for the ministers who are paid to understand and explain them, and attend to matters more within thy scope.' And then he went on to tell of a far better way to get rid of the burden that meddlesome men brought on themselves by reading that book too much—a far better and swifter way than attempting the wicket-gate. 'Thou wilt never be settled in thy mind till thou art rid of that burden, nor canst thou enjoy the blessings of wife and child as long as that burden lies so heavy upon thee.' That was so true that it made the pilgrim look up. A gentleman who can speak in that true style must know more than he says about such burdens as this of mine; and, after all, he may be able, who knows, to give me some good advice in my great straits. 'Pray, sir, open this secret to me, for I sorely stand in need of good counsel.' Let him here who has no such burden as this poor pilgrim had cast the first stone at Christian; I cannot. If one who looked like a gentleman came to me to-night and told me how I would on the spot get to a peace of conscience never to be lost again, and how I would get a heart to-night that would never any more plague and pollute me, I would be mightily tempted to forget what all my former teachers had told me and try this new Gospel. And especially if the gentleman said that the remedy was just at hand. 'Pray, sir,' said the breathless and spirit-less man, 'wilt thou, then, open this secret to me?'

The wit and the humour and the satire of the rest of the scene must be fully enjoyed over the great book itself. The village named Morality, hard by the hill; that judicious man Legality, who dwells in the first house you come at after you have turned the hill; Civility, the pretty young man that Legality hath to his son; the hospitality of the village; the low rents and the cheap provisions, and all the charities and amenities of the place,—all together make up such a picture as you cannot get anywhere out of John Bunyan. And then the pilgrim's stark folly in entering into Worldly-Wise-man's secret; his horror as the hill began to thunder and lighten and threaten to fall upon him; the sudden descent of Evangelist; and then the plain-spoken words that passed between the preacher and the pilgrim,—don't say again that the poorest of the Puritans were without letters, or that they had not their own esoteric writings full of fun and frolic; don't say that again till you are a pilgrim yourself, and have our John Bunyan for one of your classics by heart.

We are near an end, but before you depart, stand still a little, as Evangelist said to Christian, that I may show you the words of God. And first, watch yourselves well, for you all have a large piece of this worldly-wise man in yourselves. You all take something of some ancestor, remote or im-mediate, who was wise only for this world. Yes, to

be sure, for you still decline as they did, and desert
as they did, those you deem to be the weakest, and
stand with those that you suppose to be the strongest
side. *The Architect of Fortune* is perhaps too strong
meat for your stomach; but still, if you ever light
upon its powerful pages, you will surely blush in secret
to see yourself turned so completely inside out. You
may not have chosen your church wholly with an eye
to your shop; but you must admit that you see as
good and better men than you are doing that every
day. And it is a sure sign to you that you do not
yet know the plague of your own heart, unless you
know yourself to be a man more set upon the position and the praise that this world gives than you
yet are on the position and the praise that come
from God only. Set a watch on your own worldly
heart. Watch and pray, lest you also enter into
all Worldly-Wiseman's temptation. This is one of
the words of God to you.

Another word of God is this. The way of the
cross, said severe Evangelist, is odious to every
worldly-wise man; while, all the time, it is the only
way there is, and there never will be any other way
to eternal life. The only way to life is the way of
the cross. There are two crosses, indeed, on the
way to the Celestial City; there is, first, the Cross of
Christ, once for you, and then there is your cross
daily for Christ, and it takes both crosses to secure
and to assure any man that he is on the right road,
and that he will come at last to the right end.
'The Christian's great conquest over the world,'
says William Law, 'is all contained in the mystery
of Christ upon the cross. And true Christianity is

nothing else but an entire and absolute conformity to that spirit which Christ showed in the mysterious sacrifice of Himself upon the cross. Every man is only so far a Christian as he partakes of this same spirit of Christ—the same suffering spirit, the same sacrifice of himself, the same renunciation of the world, the same humility and meekness, the same patient bearing of injuries, reproaches, and contempts, the same dying to all the greatness, honours, and happiness of this world that Christ showed on the cross. We also are to suffer, to be crucified, to die, to rise with Christ, or else His crucifixion, His death, and His resurrection will profit us nothing.' This is the second word of God unto thee. And the third thing to-night is this, that though thy sin be very great, though thou hast a past life round thy neck enough to sink thee for ever out of the sight of God and all good men; a youth of sensuality now long and closely cloaked over with an after life of worldly prosperity, worldly decency, and worldly religion, all which only makes thee that whited sepulchre that Christ has in His eye when He speaks of thee with such a severe and dreadful countenance; yet if thou confess thyself to be all the whited sepulchre He sees thee to be, and yet knock at His gate in all thy rags and slime, He will immediately lay aside that severe countenance and will show thee all His goodwill. Notwithstanding all that thou hast done, and all thou still art, He will not deny His own words, or do otherwise than at once fulfil them all to thee. Ask, then, and it shall be given thee; seek, and thou shalt find; knock, and it shall be opened unto thee. And with a great goodwill,

He will say to those that stand by Him, Take away the filthy garments from him. And to thee He will say, Behold, I have caused all thine iniquity to pass from thee, and I will clothe thee with change of raiment.

VII

GOODWILL, THE GATEKEEPER

'Goodwill.'—Luke ii. 14.

O in process of time Christian got up to the gate. Now there was written over the gate, *Knock, and it shall be opened unto you.* He knocked, therefore, more than once or twice, saying, May I now enter here? when at last there came a grave person to the gate, named *Goodwill,* who asked him who was there?' The gravity of the gatekeeper was the first thing that struck the pilgrim. And it was the same thing that so struck some of the men who saw most of our Lord that they handed down to their children the true tradition that He was often seen in tears, but that no one had ever seen or heard Him laugh. The prophecy in the prophet concerning our Lord was fulfilled to the letter. He was indeed a man of sorrows, and He early and all His life long had a close acquaintance with grief. Our Lord had come into this world on a very sad errand. We are so stupefied and besotted with sin, that we have no conception how sad an errand our Lord had been sent on, and how sad a task He soon discovered it to be. To be a man without sin, a man hating sin, and hating nothing else but sin, and yet to have to spend all

His days in a world lying in sin, and in the end to have all that world of sin laid upon Him till He was Himself made sin,—how sad a task was that! Great, no doubt, as was the joy that was set before our Lord, and sure as He was of one day entering on that joy, yet the daily sight of so much sin in all men around Him, and the cross and the shame that lay right before Him, made Him, in spite of the future joy, all the Man of Sorrow Isaiah had said He would be, and made light-mindedness and laughter impossible to our Lord,—as it is, indeed, to all men among ourselves who have anything of His mind about this present world and the sin of this world, they also are men of sorrow, and of His sorrow. They, too, are acquainted with grief. Their tears, like His, will never be wiped off in this world. They will not laugh with all their heart till they laugh where He now laughs. Then it will be said of them, too, that they began to be merry. 'What was the matter with you that you did laugh in your sleep last night? asked Christiana of Mercy in the morning. I suppose you were in a dream. So I was, said Mercy, but are you sure that I laughed? Yes, you laughed heartily; but, prithee, Mercy, tell me thy dream. Well, I dreamed that I was in a solitary place and all alone, and was there bemoaning the hardness of my heart, when methought I saw one coming with wings towards me. So he came directly to me, and said, Mercy, what aileth thee? Now, when he heard my complaint, he said, Peace be to thee. He also wiped mine eyes with his handkerchief, and clad me in silver and gold; he put a chain about my neck also, and earrings in mine ears, and a beautiful crown upon my head. So he went up. I followed him till we came to a golden gate; and I thought I saw your husband there. But did I laugh? Laugh! ay, and well you might, to see yourself so well.'

But to return and begin again. Goodwill, who opened the gate, was, as we saw, a person of a very grave and commanding aspect; so much so, that in his sudden joy our pilgrim was a good deal over-awed as he looked on the countenance of the man who stood in the gate, and it was some time after-wards before he understood why he wore such a grave and almost sad aspect. But afterwards, as he went up the way, and sometimes returned in thought to the wicket-gate, he came to see very good reason why the keeper of that gate looked as he did look. The site and situation of the gate, for one thing, was of itself enough to banish all light-mindedness from the man who was stationed there. For the gatehouse stood just above the Slough of Despond, and that itself filled the air of the place with a dampness and a depression that could be felt. And then out of the downward windows of the gate, the watcher's eye always fell on the City of Destruction in the distance, and on her sister cities sitting like her daughters round about her. And that also made mirth and hilarity impossible at that gate. And then the kind of characters who came knocking all hours of the day and the night at that gate. Goodwill never saw a happy face or heard a cheerful voice from one year's end to the other. And when any one so far forgot himself as to put on an untimely confidence and self-satisfaction, the gatekeeper would soon put him through such questions as quickly sobered him if he had anything at all of the root of the matter in him. Terror, horror, despair, remorse, chased men and women up to that gate. They would often fall before his threshold more dead than alive. And then, after the gate was opened and the pilgrims pulled in, the gate had only opened on a path of such painfulness, toil, and terrible risk, that at whatever window Goodwill looked out, he always saw enough to make him and keep him a grave, if not a sad, man. It was, as he sometimes said, his meat and his drink to keep the gate open for pilgrims; but the class of men who came calling themselves pilgrims; the condition they came in; the past, that in spite of all both he and they could do, still came in through his gate after them, and went up all the way with them; their ignorance of the way, on which he could only start them; the multitudes who started, and the handfuls who held on; the many who for a time ran well, but afterwards left their bones to bleach by the wayside; and all the impossible-to-be-told troubles, dangers, sorrows, shipwrecks that certainly lay before the most steadfast and single-hearted pilgrim—all that was more than enough to give the man at the gate his grave and anxious aspect.

Not that his great gravity, with all the causes of it, ever made him a melancholy, a morose, a despairing, or even a desponding man. Far from that. The man of sorrows Himself sometimes rejoiced in spirit. Not sometimes only, but often He lifted up His heart and thanked His Father for the work His

Father had given Him to do, and for the success that had been granted to Him in the doing of it. And as often as He looked forward to the time when he should finish His work and receive His discharge, and return to His Father's house, at the thought of that He straightway forgot all His present sorrows. And somewhat so was it with Goodwill at his gate. No man could be but at bottom happy, and even joyful, who had a post like his to occupy, a gate like his to keep, and, altogether, a work like his to do. No man with his name and his nature can ever in any circumstances be really unhappy. 'Happiness is the bloom that always lies on a life of true goodness,' and this gatehouse was full of the happiness that follows on and always dwells with true goodness. Goodwill cannot have more happiness till he shuts in his last pilgrim into the Celestial City, and then himself enters in after him as a shepherd after a lost sheep.

The happy, heavenly, divine disposition of the gatekeeper was such, that it overflowed from the pilgrim who stood beside him and descended upon his wife and children who remained behind him in the doomed city. So full of love was the gate-keeper's heart, that it ran out upon Obstinate and Pliable also. His heart was so large and so hospitable, that he was not satisfied with one pilgrim received and assisted that day. How is it, he asked, that you have come here alone? Did any of your neighbours know of your coming? And why did he who came so far not come through? Alas, poor man, said Goodwill, is the celestial glory of so little

esteem with him that he counteth it not worth
running the hazards of a few difficulties to obtain it ?
Our pilgrim got a life-long lesson in goodwill to all
men at that gate that day. The gatekeeper showed
such deep and patient and genuine interest in all
the pilgrim's past history, and in all his family and
personal affairs, that Christian all his days could
never show impatience, or haste, or lack of interest
in the most long-winded and egotistical pilgrim he
ever met. He always remembered, when he was
becoming impatient, how much of his precious time
and of his loving attention his old friend Goodwill
had given to him. Our pilgrim got tired of talking
about himself long before Goodwill had ceased to
ask questions and to listen to the answers. So
much was Christian taken with the courtesy and the
kindness of Goodwill, that had it not been for his
crushing burden, he would have offered to remain in
Goodwill's house to run his errands, to light his fires,
and to sweep his floors. So much was he taken
captive with Goodwill's extraordinary kindness and
unwearied attention. And since he could not
remain at the gate, but must go on to the city of
all goodwill itself, our pilgrim set himself all his
days to copy this gatekeeper when he met with any
fellow-pilgrim who had any story that he wished to
tell. And many were the lonely and forgotten
souls that Christian cheered and helped on, not by
his gold or his silver, nor by anything else, but just
by his open ear. To listen with patience and with
attention to a fellow-pilgrim's wrongs and sorrows,
and even his smallest interests, said this Christian to
himself, is just what Goodwill so winningly did to me.

With all his goodwill the grave gatekeeper could not say that the way to the Celestial City was other than a narrow, a stringent, and a heart-searching way. 'Come,' he said, 'and I will tell thee the way thou must go.' There are many wide ways to hell, and many there be who crowd them, but there is only one way to heaven, and you will sometimes think you must have gone off it, there are so few companions ; sometimes there will be only one footprint, with here and there a stream of blood, and always as you proceed, it becomes more and more narrow, till it strips a man bare, and sometimes threatens to close upon him and crush him to the earth altogether. Our Lord in as many words tells us all that. Strive, He says, strive every day. For many shall seek to enter into the way of salvation, but because they do not early enough, and long enough, and painfully enough strive, they come short, and are shut out. Have you, then, anything in your religious life that Christ will at last accept as the striving He intended and demanded? Does your religion cause you any real effort—Christ calls it *agony*? Have you ever had, do you ever have, anything that He would so describe? What cross do you every day take up? In what thing do you every day deny yourself? Name it. Put your finger on it. Write it in cipher on the margin of your Bible. Would the most liberal judgment be able to say of you that you have any fear and trembling in the work of your salvation? If not, I am afraid there must be some mistake somewhere. There must be great guilt somewhere. At your parents' door, or at your minister's, or, if their hands are clean, then at your own. Christ has made it plain to a proverb, and John Bunyan has made it a nursery and a schoolboy story, that the way to heaven is steep and narrow and lonely and perilous. And that, remember, not a few of the first miles of the way, but all the way, and even through the dark valley itself. 'Almost all that is said in the New Testament of men's watching, giving earnest heed to themselves, running the race that is set before them, striving and agonising, fighting, putting on the whole armour of God, pressing forward, reaching forth, crying to God day and night; I say, almost all that we have in the New Testament on these subjects is spoken and directed to the saints. Where those things are applied to sinners seeking salvation once, they are spoken of the saints' prosecution of their salvation ten times' (Jonathan Edwards). If you have a life at all like that, you will be sorely tempted to think that such suffering and struggle, increasing rather than diminishing as life goes on, is a sign that you are so bad as not to be a true Christian at all. You will be tempted to think and say so. But all the time the truth is, that he who has not that labouring, striving, agonising, fearing, and trembling in himself, knows nothing at all about the religion of Christ and the way to heaven; and if he thinks he does, then that but proves him a hypocrite, a self-deceived, self-satisfied hypocrite; there is not an ounce of a true Christian in him. Says Samuel Rutherford on this matter: 'Christ commandeth His hearers to a strict and narrow way, in mortifying heart-lusts, in loving our enemy, in feeding him when he is hungry, in suffering for Christ's sake and the gospel's, in bearing His cross, in denying ourselves, in becoming humble as children, in being to all men and at all times meek and lowly in heart.' Let any man lay all that intelligently and imaginatively alongside of his own daily life. Let him name some such heart-lust. Let him name also some enemy, and ask himself what it is to love that man, and to feed him in his hunger; what it is in which he is called to suffer for Christ's sake and the gospel's, in his reputation, in his property, in his business, in his feelings. Let him put his finger on something in which he is every day to deny himself, and to be humble and teachable, and to keep himself out of sight like a little child; and if that man does not find out how narrow and heart-searching the way to heaven is, he will be the first who has so found his way thither. No, no; be not deceived. Deceive not yourself, and let no man deceive you. God is not mocked, neither are His true saints. 'Would to God I were back in my pulpit but for one Sabbath,' said a dying minister in Aberdeen. 'What would you do?' asked a brother minister at his bedside. 'I would preach to the people the difficulty of salvation,' he said. All which things are told, not for purposes of debate or defiance, but to comfort and instruct God's true people who are finding salvation far more difficult than anybody had ever told them it would be. Comfort My people, saith your God. Speak comfortably to My people. Come, said Goodwill, and I will teach thee about the way thou must go. Look before thee, dost thou see that narrow way? That is the way thou must go. And then thou mayest always distinguish the right way from the wrong. The wrong is crooked and wide, and the right is straight as a rule can make it,—straight and narrow.

Goodwill said all that in order to direct and to comfort the pilgrim; but that was not all that this good man said with that end. For, when Christian asked him if he could not help him off with his burden that was upon his back, he told him : ' As to thy burden, be content to bear it until thou comest to the place of deliverance, for there it will fall from thy back of itself.' Get you into the straight and narrow way, says Goodwill, with his much experience of the ways and fortunes of true pilgrims; get you sure into the right way, and leave your burden to God. He appoints the place of deliverance, and it lies before thee. The place of thy deliverance cannot be behind thee, and it is not in my house, else thy burden would have been already off. But it is before thee. Be earnest, therefore, in the way. Look not behind thee. Go not into any crooked way ; and one day, before you know, and when you are not pulling at it, your burden will fall off of itself. Be content to bear it till then, says bold and honest Goodwill, speaking so true to pilgrim experience. Yes ; be content, O ye people of God, crying with this pilgrim for release from your burden of guilt, and no less those of you who are calling with Paul for release from the still more bitter and crushing burden made up of combined guilt and corruption. Be content till the place and the time of deliverance ; nay, even under your burden and your bonds be glad, as Paul was, and go up the narrow way, still chanting to yourself,

I thank God through Jesus Christ our Lord. It is only becoming that a great sinner should tarry the Lord's leisure; all the more that the greatest sinner may be sure the Lord will come, and will not tarry. The time is long, but the thing is sure.

And now two lessons from Goodwill's gate :—

1. The gate was shut when Christian came up to it, and no one was visible anywhere about it. The only thing visible was the writing over the gate which told all pilgrims to knock. Now, when we come up to the same gate we are disappointed and discouraged that the gatekeeper is not standing already upon his doorstep and his arms round our neck. We knelt to-day in secret prayer, and there was only our bed or our chair visible before us. There was no human being, much less to all appearance any Divine Presence, in the place. And we prayed a short, indeed, but a not unearnest prayer, and then we rose up and came away disappointed because no one appeared. But look at him who is now inheriting the promises. He knocked, says his history, more than once or twice. That is to say, he did not content himself with praying one or two seconds and then giving over, but he continued in prayer till the gatekeeper came. And as he knocked, he said, so loud and so impatient that all those in the gatehouse could hear him,

'May I now enter here? Will he within
Open to sorry me, though I have been
A wandering rebel? Then shall I
Not fail to sing his lasting praise on high.'

2. 'We make no objections against any,' said

Goodwill; 'notwithstanding all that they have done before they come hither, they are in no wise cast out.' He told me all things that ever I did, said the woman of Samaria, telling her neighbours about our Lord's conversation with her. And, somehow, there was something in the gatekeeper's words that called back to Christian, if not all the things he had ever done, yet from among them the worst things he had ever done. They all rose up black as hell before his eyes as the gatekeeper did not name them at all, but only said 'notwithstanding all that thou hast done.' Christian never felt his past life so black, or his burden so heavy, or his heart so broken, as when Goodwill just said that one word 'notwithstanding.' 'We make no objections against any; notwithstanding all that they have done before they come hither, they are in no wise cast out.'

VIII

THE INTERPRETER

'An interpreter, one among a thousand.'—*Elihu.*

E come to-night to the Interpreter's House. And since every minister of the gospel is an interpreter, and every evangelical church is an interpreter's house, let us gather up some of the precious lessons to ministers and to people with which this passage of the *Pilgrim's Progress* so much abounds.

1. In the first place, then, I observe that the House of the Interpreter stands just beyond the Wicket Gate. In the whole topography of the *Pilgrim's Progress* there lies many a deep lesson. The church that Mr. Worldly-Wiseman supported, and on the communion roll of which he was so determined to have our pilgrim's so unprepared name, stood far down on the other side of Goodwill's gate. It was a fine building, and it had an eloquent man for its minister, and the whole service was an attraction and an enjoyment to all the people of the place; but our Interpreter was never asked to show any of his significant things there; and, indeed, neither minister nor people would have understood him had he ever done so. And had any of the parishioners from below the gate ever by

any chance stumbled into the Interpreter's house,
his most significant rooms would have had no
significance to them. Both he and his house
would have been a mystery and an offence to
Worldly-Wiseman, his minister, and his fellow-
worshippers. John Bunyan has the clear warrant
both of Jesus Christ and the Apostle Paul for the
place on which he has planted the Interpreter's
house. 'It is given to you,' said our Lord to His
disciples, 'to know the mysteries of the Kingdom
of Heaven, but to them it is not given.' And Paul
tells us that 'the natural man receiveth not the
things of the Spirit of God, for they are foolishness
unto him : neither can he know them, because they
are spiritually discerned.' And, accordingly, no
reader of the *Pilgrim's Progress* will really
understand what he sees in the Interpreter's
House, unless he is already a man of a spiritual
mind. Intelligent children enjoy the pictures
and the people that are set before them in this
illustrated house, but they must become the
children of God, and must be well on in the life of
God, before they will be able to say that the house
next the gate has been a profitable and a
helpful house to them. All that is displayed here—
all the furniture and all the vessels, all the ornaments and all the employments and all the people
of the Interpreter's House—is fitted and intended
to be profitable as well as interesting to pilgrims
only. No man has any real interest in the things
of this house, or will take any abiding profit out of
it, till he is fairly started on the upward road. In
his former life, and while still on the other side of

the gate, our pilgrim had no interest in such things as he is now to see and hear; and if he had seen and heard them in his former life, he would not, with all the Interpreter's explanation, have understood them. As here among ourselves to-night, they who will understand and delight in the things they hear in this house to-night are those only who have really begun to live a religious life. The realities of true religion are now the most real things in life to them; they love divine things now; and since they began to love divine things, you cannot entertain them better than by exhibiting and explaining divine things to them. There is no house in all the earth, after the gate itself, that is more dear to the true pilgrim heart than just the Interpreter's House. 'I was glad when it was said to me, Let us go into the house of the Lord. Peace be within thy walls, and prosperity within thy palaces.'

2. And besides being built on the very best spot in all the land for its owner's purposes, every several room in that great house was furnished and fitted up for the entertainment and instruction of pilgrims. Every inch of that capacious and many-chambered house was given up to the delectation of pilgrims. The public rooms were thrown open for their convenience and use at all hours of the day and night, and the private rooms were kept retired and secluded for such as sought retirement and seclusion. There were dark rooms also with iron cages in them, till Christian and his companions came out of those terrible places, bringing with them an everlasting caution to watchfulness and a sober mind. There were rooms also given up to vile and sordid uses.

One room there was full of straws and sticks and
dust, with an old man who did nothing else day nor
night but wade about among the straws and sticks
and dust, and rake it all into little heaps, and then
sit watching lest any one should overturn them.
And then, strange to tell it, and not easy to get to
the full significance of it, the bravest room in all the
house had absolutely nothing in it but a huge, ugly,
poisonous spider hanging to the wall with her hands.
'Is there but one spider in all this spacious room?'
asked the Interpreter. And the water stood in
Christiana's eyes; she had come by this time thus
far on her journey also. She was a woman of a
quick apprehension, and the water stood in her eyes
at the Interpreter's question, and she said: 'Yes,
Lord, there is here more than one. Yea, and spiders
whose venom is far more destructive than that which
is in her.' The Interpreter then looked pleasantly
on her, and said: 'Thou hast said the truth.' This
made Mercy blush, and the boys to cover their
faces, for they all began now to understand the
riddle. 'This is to show you,' said the Interpreter,
'that however full of the venom of sin you may be,
yet you may, by the hand of faith, lay hold of, and
dwell in the best room that belongs to the King's
House above.' Then they all seemed to be glad,
but the water stood in their eyes. A wall also stood
apart on the grounds of the house with an always
dying fire on one side of it, while a man on the
other side of the wall continually fed the fire
through hidden openings in the wall. A whole
palace stood also on the grounds, the inspection of
which so kindled our pilgrim's heart, that he refused

to stay here any longer, or to see any more sights—
so much had he already seen of the evil of sin and
of the blessedness of salvation. Not that he had
seen as yet the half of what that house held for the
instruction of pilgrims. Only, time would fail us to
visit the hen and her chickens; the butcher killing
a sheep and pulling her skin over her ears, and she
lying still under his hands and taking her death
patiently; also the garden with the flowers all
diverse in stature, and quality, and colour, and
smell, and virtue, and some better than some, and all
where the gardener had set them, there they stand,
and quarrel not with one another. The robin-red-
breast also, so pretty of note and colour and carriage,
but instead of bread and crumbs, and such like harm-
less matter, with a great spider in his mouth. A tree
also, whose inside was rotten, and yet it grew and
had leaves. So they went on their way and sang:

> 'This place hath been our second stage,
>   Here have we heard and seen
> Those good things that from age to age
>   To others hid have been.
> The butcher, garden, and the field,
>   The robin and his bait,
> Also the rotten tree, doth yield
>   Me argument of weight;
> To move me for to watch and pray,
>   To strive to be sincere,
> To take my cross up day by day,
>   And serve the Lord with fear.'

The significant rooms of that divine house instruct
us also that all the lessons requisite for our salvation
are not to be found in any one scripture or in any one
sermon, but that all that is required by any pilgrim
or any company of pilgrims should all be found

in every minister's ministry as he leads his flock on from one Sabbath-day to another, rightly dividing the word of truth. Our ministers should have something in their successive sermons for everybody. Something for the children, something for the slow-witted and the dull of understanding, and something specially suited for those who are of a quick apprehension; something at one time to make the people smile, at another time to make them blush, and at another time to make the water stand in their eyes.

3. And, then, the Interpreter's life was as full of work as his house was of entertainment and instruction. Not only so, but his life, it was well known, had been quite as full of work before he had a house to work for as ever it had been since. The Interpreter did nothing else but continually preside over his house and all that was in it and around it, and it was all gone over and seen to with his own eyes and hands every day. He had been present at the laying of every stone and beam of that solid and spacious house of his. There was not a pin nor a loop of its furniture, there was not a picture on its walls, nor a bird nor a beast in its woods and gardens, that he did not know all about and could not hold discourse about. And then, after he had taken you all over his house, with its significant rooms and woods and gardens, he was full all suppertime of all wise saws and witty proverbs. 'One leak will sink a ship,' he said that night, 'and one sin will destroy a sinner.' And all their days the pilgrims remembered that word from the Interpreter's lips, and they often said it to themselves as

they thought of their own besetting sin. Now, if it is indeed so, that every gospel minister is an interpreter, and every evangelical church an interpreter's house, what an important passage this is for all those who are proposing and preparing to be ministers. Let them reflect upon it: what a house this is that the Interpreter dwells in; how early and how long ago he began to lay out his grounds and to build his house upon them; how complete in all its parts it is, and how he still watches and labours to have it more complete. Understandest thou what thou here readest? it is asked of all ministers, young and old, as they turn over John Bunyan's pungent pages. And every new room, every new bird, and beast, and herb, and flower makes us blush for shame as we contrast our own insignificant and ill-furnished house with the noble house of the Interpreter. Let all our students who have not yet fatally destroyed themselves and lost their opportunity lay the Interpreter's House well to heart. Let them be students not in idle name only, as so many are, but in intense reality, as so few are. Let them read everything that bears upon the Bible, and let them read nothing that does not. They have not the time nor the permission. Let them be content to be men of one book. Let them give themselves wholly to the interpretation of divine truth as its riddles are set in nature and in man, in scripture, in providence, and in spiritual experience. Let them store their memories at college with all sacred truth, and with all secular truth that can be made sacred. And if their memories are weak and treacherous, let them be quiet under God's will in that, and all the more labour to make up in other ways for that defect, so that they may have always something to say to the purpose when their future people come up to church hungry for instruction and comfort and encouragement. Let them look around and see the sin that sinks the ship of so many ministers; and let them begin while yet their ship is in the yard and see that she is fitted up and furnished, stored and stocked, so that she shall in spite of sure storms and sunken rocks deliver her freight in the appointed haven. When they are lying in bed of a Sabbath morning, let them forecast the day when they shall have to give a strict account of their eight years of golden opportunity among the churches, and the classes, and the societies, and the libraries of our university seats. Let them be able to name some great book, ay, more than one great book, they mastered, for every year of their priceless and irredeemable student life. Let them all their days have old treasure-houses that they filled full with scholarship and with literature and with all that will minister to a congregation's many desires and necessities, collected and kept ready from their student days. 'Meditate upon these things; give thyself wholly up to them, that thy profiting may appear unto all.'

4. And then with a sly stroke at us old ministers, our significant author points out to us how much better furnished the Interpreter's House was by the time Christiana and the boys visited it compared with that early time when Christian was entertained in it. Our pilgrim got far more in the Interpreter's

House of delight and instruction than he could carry out of it, but that did not tempt the Interpreter to sit down and content himself with taking all his future pilgrims into the same room, and showing them the same pictures, and repeating to them the same explanations. No, for he reflected that each coming pilgrim would need some new significant room to himself, and therefore, as soon as he got one pilgrim off his hands, he straightway set about building and furnishing new rooms, putting up new pictures, and replenishing his woods and his waters with new beasts and birds and fishes. I am ashamed, he said, that I had so little to show when I first opened my gates to receive pilgrims, and I do not know why they came to me as they did. I was only a beginner in these things when my first visitor came to my gates. Let every long-settled, middle-aged, and even grey-headed minister read the life of the Interpreter at this point and take courage and have hope. Let it teach us all to break some new ground in the field of divine truth with every new year. Let it teach us all to be students all our days. Let us buy, somehow, the poorest and the oldest of us, some new and first-rate book every year. Let us not indeed shut up altogether our old rooms if they ever had anything significant in them, but let us add now a new wing to our spiritual house, now a new picture to its walls, and now a new herb to its gardens. Resolved,' wrote Jonathan Edwards, 'that as old men have seldom any advantage of new discoveries, because these are beside a way of thinking they have been long used to ; resolved, therefore, if ever I live to

years, that I will be impartial to hear the reasons
of all pretended discoveries, and receive them,
if rational, how long soever I have been used to
another way of thinking.'

5. The fickle, frivolous, volatile character of so
many divinity students is excellently hit off by
Bunyan in our pilgrim's impatience to be out of the
Interpreter's House. No sooner had he seen one
or two of the significant rooms than this easily
satisfied student was as eager to get out of that
house as he had been to get in. Twice over the
wise and learned Interpreter had to beg and beseech this ignorant and impulsive pilgrim to stop
and get another lesson in the religious life before
he left the great school-house. All our professors
of divinity and all our ministers understand the
parable at this point only too well. Their students
are eager to get into their classes; like our pilgrim,
they have heard the fame of this and that teacher,
and there is not standing-room in the class for the
first weeks of the session. But before Christmas
there is room enough for strangers, and long before
the session closes, half the students are counting the
weeks and plotting to petition the Assembly against
the length and labour of the curriculum. Was there
ever a class that was as full and attentive at the end
of the session as it was at the beginning? Never
since our poor human nature was so stricken with
laziness and shallowness and self-sufficiency. But
what is the chaff to the wheat? It is the wheat
that deserves and repays the husbandman's love and
labour. When Plato looked up from his desk in the
Academy, after reading and expounding one of his

greatest Dialogues, he found only one student left
in the class-room, but then, that student was Aristotle. 'Now let me go,' said Christian. 'Nay, stay,'
said the Interpreter, 'till I have showed thee a little
more.' 'Sir, is it not time for me to go?' 'Do
tarry till I show thee just one thing more.'

6.   'Here have I seen things rare and profitable,
                .   .   .   Then let me be
            Thankful, O good Interpreter, to thee.'

Sydney Smith, with his usual sagacity, says that
the last vice of the pulpit is to be uninteresting.
Now, the Interpreter's House had this prime virtue
in it, that it was all interesting. Do not our children
beg of us on Sabbath nights to let them see the
Interpreter's show once more; it is so inexhaustibly
and unfailingly interesting? It is only stupid men
and women who ever weary of it. But, 'profitable'
was the one and universal word with which all the
pilgrims left the Interpreter's House. 'Rare and
pleasant,' they said, and sometimes 'dreadful;' but
it was always 'profitable.' Now, how seldom do we
hear our people at the church door step down into
the street saying, 'profitable'? If they said that
oftener, their ministers would study profit more than
they do. The people say 'able,' or 'not at all able';
'eloquent,' or 'stammering and stumbling'; 'excellent' in style and manner and accent, or the
opposite of all that; and their ministers, to please
the people and to earn their approval, labour after
these approved things. But if the people only said
that the prayers and the preaching were profitable
and helpful, even when they too seldom are, then
our preachers would set the profit of the people far

more before them both in selecting and treating and
delivering their Sabbath-day subjects. A lady on
one occasion said to her minister, 'Sir, your preaching
does my soul good.' And her minister never forgot
the grave and loving look with which that was said.
Not only did he never forget it, but often when
selecting his subject, and treating it, and delivering
it, the question would rise in his heart and conscience,
Will that do my friend's soul any good? 'Rare and
profitable,' said the pilgrim as he left the gate; and
hearing that sent the Interpreter back with new
spirit and new invention to fill his house of still
more significant, rare, and profitable things than
ever before. 'Meditate on these things,' said Paul
to Timothy his son in the gospel, 'that thy profiting
may appear unto all.' 'Thou art a minister of the
word,' wrote the learned William Perkins beside his
name on all his books, 'mind thy business.'

IX

PASSION

A man subject to like passions as we are.'—*James* v. 17.

THAT was a very significant room in the Interpreter's House where our pilgrim saw Passion and Patience sitting each one in his chair. Passion was a young lad who seemed to our pilgrim to be much discontented. He was never satisfied. He would have all his good things now. His governor would have him wait for his best things till the beginning of next year; but no, he will have them all now. And then, when he had got all his good things, he soon lavished and wasted them all till he had nothing left but rags. Then said Christian to the Interpreter, 'Expound this matter more fully to me.' So he said, 'Those two lads are figures; Passion, of the men of this world; and Patience of the men of that which is to come.' 'Then I perceive,' said Christian, ''tis not best to covet things that are now, but to wait for things to come.' You say truth,' replied the Interpreter, 'for the things that are seen are temporal, but the things that are not seen are eternal.'

Now, from the texts that I have taken out of James and out of this so significant room in the Interpreter's House, let me try to tell you something profitable, if so it may be, about passion; the nature of it, the place it holds, and the part it performs both in human nature and in the life and the character of a Christian man.

The name of Passion has already told us his nature, his past life, and his present character. The whole nomenclature of *The Pilgrim's Progress* and of *The Holy War* is composed on the divine, original, and natural principle of embodying the nature of a man in his name. God takes His own names to Himself on that principle. The Creator gave Adam his name also on that same principle; and then Adam gave their names to all cattle, to the fowls of the air, and to every beast of the field on the same principle on which he had got his own name. And so it was at first with all the Bible names of men and of nations of men. Their name contained their nature. And John Bunyan was such a student of the Bible, and of no other book but the Bible, that all his best books are all full, like the Bible, of the most descriptive and suggestive names. As soon as Bunyan tells us the name of some new acquaintance or fellow-traveller, we already know him, so exactly is his nature put into his name. And thus it is that when we stop for a moment at the door of this little significant room in the Interpreter's House and ask ourselves the meaning of the name Passion, we see at once where we are and what we have here before us. For a 'passion' is just some excitement or agitation of the mind caused by some outward thing acting on the mind. The inward world of the mind and heart of man, and this outward world down into which God has placed man, instantly and continually respond to one another. And what are called, with so much correctness and propriety, our passions, are just those inward responses, excitements, and agitations that the outward world causes in the inward world when those two worlds meet together. 'Passion' and 'perturbation' are the old classical names that the ancient philosophers and moralists gave to what they felt in themselves as their minds and their hearts were affected by the world of men and things around them. And they used to illustrate their teaching on the subject of the passions by the figure of a storm at sea. They said that it was because God had made the sea sensitive and responsive to the winds that blew over it that a storm at sea ever arose. The storm did not arise and the ships were not wrecked by anything from within the sea itself; it was the outward world of the winds striking against the quiet and inward world of the waters that roused the storms and sank the ships. And with that illustration well printed in the minds and imaginations of their scholars the old moralists felt their work among their scholars was already all but done. For, so full of adaptation and appeal is the whole outward world to the mind and heart of man, and so sensitive and instantly responsive is the mind and heart of man to all the approaches of the outward world, that the mind and heart of man are constantly full of all kinds of passions, both bad and good. And, then, this is our present life of probation and opportunity, that all our passions are placed within us and are committed and entrusted to us as so many first elements and so much unformed material out of which we are summoned to build up our life and to shape and complete our character. The springs of all our actions are in our passions. All our activities in life, trace them all up to their source, and they will all be found to run up into the wellhead of our passions. All our virtues are cut as with a chisel out of our passions, and all our vices are just the disorders and rebellions of our passions. Our several passions, as they lie still asleep in our hearts, have as yet no moral character; they are only the raw material, so to speak, of moral character. Our passions are the life and the riches and the ornaments of human nature, and it is only because human nature in its present estate is so corrupt and disordered and degraded, that the otherwise so honourable name of passion has such a sinister sound to us. And the full regeneration and restitution of human nature will be accomplished when every several passion is in its right place, and when reason and conscience and the Spirit of God shall inspire and rule and regulate all that is within us.

> ' On life's vast ocean diversely we sail,
> Reason the card, but passion is the gale.'

And not Elijah only, as James says, and not Paul and Barnabas only, as they themselves said, were men of like passions with ourselves, but our Lord Himself was a man of like passions with us also. He took to Himself a true body, full of all the appetites of the body, and a reasonable soul, full of all the affections, passions and emotions of the soul. Only, in Him reason and conscience and the law and the Spirit of God were the card and the compass according to which He steered His life. We have all our ruling passion, and our Lord also had His. As His disciples saw His ruling passion kindled in His heart and coming out in His life, they remembered that it was written of Him in an old Messianic psalm: 'The zeal of Thine house hath eaten me up.' They were all eaten up of their ruling passions also. One of ambition, one of emulation, one of avarice, and so on,—each several disciple was eaten up of his own besetting sin. But they all saw that it was not so with their Master. He was eaten up always and wholly of the zeal of His Father's house, and of absolute surrender and devotion to His Father's service, till His ruling passion was seen to be as strong in His death as it had been in His life. The Laird of Brodie's Diary has repeatedly been of great use to us in these inward matters, and his words on this subject are well worth repeating. 'We poor creatures,' he says, 'are commanded by our affections and passions. They are not at our command. But the Holy One doth exercise all His attributes at His own will; they are at His command; they are not passions nor perturbations in His mind, though they transport us. When I would hate, I cannot. When I would love, I cannot. When I would grieve, I cannot. When I would desire, I cannot. But it is the better for us that all is as He wills it to be.'

And now, to come still closer home, let us look for a moment or two at some of our own ruling and tyrannising passions. And let us look first at self-

love—that master-passion in every human heart.
Let us give self-love the first place in the inventory
and catalogue of our passions, because it has the
largest place in all our hearts and lives. Nay, not
only has self-love the largest place of any of the
passions of our hearts, but it is out of self-love that
all our other evil passions spring. It is out of this
parent passion that all the poisonous brood of our
other evil passions are born. The whole fall and ruin
and misery of our present human nature lies in this,
that in every human being self-love has taken, in
addition to its own place, the place of the love of
God and of the love of man also. We naturally now
love nothing and no one but ourselves. And as long
as self-love is in the ascendant in our hearts, all the
passions that are awakened in us by our self-love
will be selfish with its selfishness, inhumane with its
inhumanity, and ungodly with its ungodliness. And
it is to kill and extirpate our so passionate self-love
that is the end and aim of all God's dealings with
us in this world. All that God is doing with us and
for us in providence and in grace, in the world and
in the church,—it is all to cure us of this deadly
disease of self-love. We may never have had that
told us before, and we may not like it, and we may
not believe it; but there can be no better proof of
the truth of what is now said than just this, that we
do not like it and will not have it. Self-love will
not let us listen to the truth about ourselves; it
puts us in a passion both against the truth and
against him who tells the truth, as the history of the
truth abundantly testifies. Yes, your indignant protest is quite true. Self-love has her divine rights,—

no doubt she has. But you are not commanded to attend to them. Your self-love will look after herself. She will manage to have her full share of what is right and proper for any passion to possess even after she cries out that she is trampled upon and despoiled. My brethren, till you begin to crucify yourselves and to pluck up your self-love by the roots, you will never know what a cruel and hopeless task the Christian life is—I do not say the Christian profession. Nor, on the other hand, will you ever discover what a noble task it is—what a divine task and how divinely assisted and divinely recompensed. You will not know what a kennel of hell-hounds your own heart is till you have long sought to enter it and cleanse it out. And after you have done your utmost, and your best, death will hurry you away from your but half-accomplished task. Only, in that case you will be able to die in the hope that what is impossible with man is possible with God, as promised by Him, and that He will not leave your soul in hell, but will perfect that good thing which alone concerneth you, even your everlasting deliverance from all sinful self-love.

And if self-love is the fruitful mother of all our passions, then sensuality is surely her eldest son. Indeed, so shallow are we, and so shallow are our words, that when we speak of sinful passion most men instantly think of sensuality. There are so many seductive things that appeal to our appetites, and our appetites are so easily awakened, and are so imperious when they are awakened, that when passion is spoken about, few men think of the soul, all men think instantly of the body. And no wonder. For, stupid and besotted as we are, we must all at some time of our life have felt the bondage and degradation of the senses. Passion in the Interpreter's House had soon nothing left but rags. And in this house to-night there are many men whose consciences and hearts and characters are all in such rags from sensual sin, that when the Scriptures speak of uncleanness, or rags, or corruption, their thoughts flee at once to sensual sin and its conscience-rending results. Cease from sensuality, said Cicero, for if once you give your minds up to sensuality, you will never be able to think of anything else.

Ambition, emulation, and envy are the leading members of a whole prolific family of satanic passions in the human heart. Indeed, these passions, taken along with their kindred passions of hatred and ill-will, are, in our Lord's words, the very lusts of the devil himself. The Jews hated our Lord the more for what He said about these detestable passions, but His own disciples love Him only the more that He so well knows the evil affections of their hearts, and so well describes and denounces them. Anybody can denounce sensual sin, and everybody will understand and approve. But spiritual sin,—ambition and emulation and envy and ill-will—these things are more easy to denounce than they are to detect and describe, and more easy to detect and describe than they are to cast out. These sins seem rather to multiply and to strike a deeper root when you begin to cast them out. What an utterly and abominably evil passion is envy which is awakened not by bad things but by the best things! That another man's talents, attainments, praises, rewards should kindle it, and that the blame, the depreciation, the hurt that another man suffers should satisfy it,—what a piece of very hell must that be in the human heart! What more do we need than just a little envy in our hearts to make us prostrate penitents before God and man all our days? What more doctrine, argument, proof, authority, persuasion should a sane man need beyond a little envy in his heart at his best friend to make him an evangelical believer and an evangelical preacher? How, in the name of wonder, is it that men can be so ignorant of the plague of their own hearts as to remain indifferent, and, much more, hostile, to the gospel of love and holiness? Pride, also,—what a hateful and intolerable passion is that! How stone-blind to his own state must that sinner be whose heart is filled with pride, and how impossible it is for that man to make any real progress in any kind of truth or goodness! And resentment,—what a deep-seated, long-lived, and suicidal passion is that! How it hunts down him it hates, and how surely it shuts the door of salvation against him who harbours it! Forgive us our debts, the resentful man says in his prayer, as we forgive our debtors. And detraction,—how some men's ink-horns are filled with detraction for ink, and how it drops from their tongue like poison! At their every word a reputation dies. Life and all its opportunities of doing good and having good done to us is laid like a bag of treasure at our feet, but, like the prodigal son in the Interpreter's House, with all those passions raging in our own hearts at other men, and in other men's hearts at us, we have

soon nothing left us but rags. God be thanked for
every man here who sees and feels that he has
nothing left him but rags; and, still more, thanks
for all those who see and feel how, by their bad
passions, sensual and spiritual, they have left on
other people nothing but rags.

Now, from all this let us lay it to heart that our
sanctification and salvation lie in our mastery over
all these and over many other passions that have not
even been named. He is an accepted saint of God,
who, taking his and other people's rags to God's
mercy every day, every day also in God's strength
grapples with, bridles, and tames his own wild and
ungodly passions. Be not deceived, my friends; he
alone is a saint of God who is a sanctified man; and
his passions,—as they are the spring of his actions, so
they are the sphere and seat of his sanctification.
Be not deceived; that man, and no other manner
of man, is, or ever will be, a partaker of God's salvation. You often hear me recommending those
students who have first to subdue their own passions
and then the passions of those who hear them to
study Jonathan Edwards' ethical and spiritual
writings. Well, just at this present point, to show
you how well that great man practised what he
preached, let me read to you a few lines from his
biographer: 'Few men,' says Henry Rogers, 'ever
attained a more complete mastery over their passions
than Jonathan Edwards did. This was partly owing
to the ascendency of his intellect; partly, and in
a still greater degree, to the elevation of his piety.
For the subjugation of his passions he was no doubt
very greatly indebted to the prodigious superiority

of his reason. Such was the commanding attitude his reason assumed, and such the tremendous power with which it controlled the whole man, that any insurrection among his senses was hopeless; they had their tenure only by doing fealty and homage to his intellect. Those other and more dangerous enemies, because more subtle and more spiritual, such as pride, vanity, wrath, and envy, which lurk in the inmost recesses of our nature, and some of which have such affinities for a genius like that of Edwards, yield not to such exorcism. Such more powerful kind of demons go not forth but by prayer and fasting; to their complete mortification, therefore, Edwards brought incessant watchfulness and devotion; and seldom, assuredly, have they been more nearly expelled from the bosom of a depraved intelligence.' We shall be in the best company, both intellectually and spiritually, if we work out our own salvation among the sinful passions of our depraved hearts. And then, as life goes on, and we continue in well-doing, we shall be able to measure and register our growth in grace best by watching the effect of outward temptations upon our still sinful and but half-sanctified hearts. And among much to be humbled for, and much to make us fear and tremble for the issue, we shall, from time to time, have a good conscience and a holy and humble joy that this passion and that is at last showing some signs of crucifixion and mortification. And thus that death to sin shall gradually set in which shall issue at last in an everlasting life unto holiness.

'Then will I sprinkle clean water upon you, and

ye shall be clean : from all your filthiness, and from all your idols will I cleanse you. A new heart also will I give you, and a new spirit will I put within you. . . . Behold, I have caused thine iniquity to pass from thee, and I will clothe thee with change of raiment. In that day there shall be a fountain opened to the house of David, and to the inhabitants of Jerusalem, for sin and for uncleanness. . . . Bring forth the best robe and put it upon him, for this my son was dead, and is alive again; he was lost, and is found. . . . What are these that are arrayed in white robes, and whence came they ? These are they which came out of great tribulation, and have washed their robes, and made them white in the blood of the Lamb.'

X

PATIENCE

'In your patience possess ye your souls.' (Revised Version : 'In your patience ye shall win your souls.')—*Our Lord*.

 SAW moreover in my dream that the Interpreter took the pilgrim by the hand, and had him into a little room, where sate two little children, each one in his chair. The name of the eldest was Passion and of the other Patience. Passion seemed to be much discontent, but Patience was very quiet. Then Christian asked, What is the reason of the discontent of Passion? The Interpreter answered, The governor of them would have him stay for his best things till the beginning of the next year; but he will have all now. But Patience is willing to wait.'

Passion and Patience, like Esau and Jacob, are twin-brothers. And their names, like their natures, spring up from the same root. 'Patience,' says Crabb in his *English Synonyms,* 'comes from the active participle to suffer; while passion comes from the passive participle of the same verb; and hence the difference between the two names. Patience signifies suffering from an active principle, a determination to suffer; while passion signifies what is suffered from want of power to prevent the suffering.

Patience, therefore, is always taken in a good sense, and Passion always in a bad sense.' So far this excellent etymologist. This is, therefore, another case of blessing and cursing proceeding out of the same mouth, and of the same fountain sending forth at the same place both sweet water and bitter.

Our Lord tells us in this striking text that our very souls by reason of sin are not our own. He tells us that we have lost hold of our souls before we have as yet come to know that we have souls. We only discover that we have souls after we have lost them. And our Lord,—our best, indeed our only, authority in the things of the soul,—here tells us that it is only by patience that we shall ever win back our lost souls. More, far more, is needed to the winning back of a lost soul than its owner's patience, and our Lord knew that to His cost. But that is not His point with us to-night. His sole point with each one of us to-night is our personal part in the conquest and redemption of our sin-enslaved souls. He who has redeemed our souls with His own blood tells us with all plainness of speech, that His blood will be shed in vain, as far as we are concerned, unless we add to His atoning death our own patient life. Every human life, as our Lord looks at it, and would have us look at it, is a vast field of battle in which a soul is lost or won ; little as we think of it or will believe it, in His sight every trial, temptation, provocation, insult, injury, and all kinds and all degrees of pain and suffering, are all so many divinely appointed opportunities afforded us for the reconquest and recovery of our souls. Some-times faith is summoned into the battle-field, sometimes hope, sometimes self-denial, sometimes prayer, sometimes one grace and sometimes another; but as with the sound of a trumpet the Captain of our salvation here summons Patience to the forefront of the fight.

1. To begin with, how much impatience we are all from time to time guilty of in our family life. Among the very foundations of our family life how much impatience the husband often exhibits toward the wife, and the wife toward her husband. Patience is the very last grace they look forward to having any need of when they are still dreaming about their married life; but, in too many cases, they have not well entered on that life, when they find that they need no grace of God so much as just patience, if the yoke of their new life is not to gall them beyond endurance. However many good qualities of mind and heart and character any husband or wife may have, no human being is perfect, and most of us are very far from being perfect. When, therefore, we are closely and indissolubly joined to another life and another will, it is no wonder that sometimes the ill-fitting yoke eats into a lifelong sore. We have all many defects in our manners, in our habits, and in our constitutional ways of thinking and speaking and acting,—defects that tempt those who live nearest us to fall into annoyances with us that sometimes deepen into dislike, and even positive disgust, till it has been seen, in some extreme cases, that home-life has become a very prison-house, in which the impatient prisoner chafes and jibs and strikes out as he does nowhere else. Now, when any unhappy man or

woman wakens up to discover how different life is now to be from what it once promised to become, let them know that all their past blindness, and precipitancy, and all the painful results of all that, may yet be made to work together for good. In your patience with one another, says our Lord, you will make a conquest of your adverse lot, and of your souls to the bargain. Say to yourselves, therefore, that perfection, faultlessness, and absolute satisfaction are not to be found in this world. And say also that since you have not brought perfection to your side of the house any more than your partner has to his side, you are not so foolish as to expect perfection in return for such imperfection. You have your own share of what causes fireside silence, aversion, disappointment, and dislike; and, with God's help, say that you will patiently submit to what may not now be mended. And then, the sterner the battle the nobler will the victory be; and the lonelier the fight, the more honour to him who flinches not from it. In your patience possess ye your souls.

What a beautiful, instructive, and even impressive sight it is to see a nurse patiently cherishing her children! How she has her eye and her heart at all their times upon them, till she never has any need to lay her hand upon them! Passion has no place in her little household, because patience fills all its own place and the place of passion too. What a genius she displays in her talks to her children! How she cheats their little hours of temptation, and tides them over the rough places that her eye sees lying like sunken rocks before her little ship! How skilfully she stills and heals their impulsive little passions by her sudden and absorbing surprise at some miracle in a picture-book, or some astonishing sight under her window! She has a thousand occupations also for her children, and each of them with a touch of enterprise and adventure and benevolence in it. She is so full of patience herself, that the little gusts of passion are soon over in her presence; and the sunshine is soon back brighter than ever in her little paradise. And, over and above her children rising up and calling her blessed, what wounds she escapes in her own heart and memory by keeping her patient hands from ever wounding her children! What peace she keeps in the house, just by having peace always within herself! Paul can find no better figure wherewith to set forth God's marvellous patience with Israel during her fretful childhood in the wilderness, than just that of such a nurse among her provoking children. And we see the deep hold that same touching and instructive sight had taken of the apostle's heart as he returns to it again to the Thessalonians : 'We were gentle among you, even as a nurse cherisheth her children. So, being affectionately desirous of you, we were willing to have imparted unto you, not the gospel of God only, but also our own souls, because ye were dear unto us.' What a school of divine patience is every man's own family at home if he only were teachable, observant, and obedient !

2. Clever, quick-witted, and, themselves, much-gifted men, are terribly intolerant of slow and stupid men, as they call them. But the many-talented man makes a great mistake here, and falls into a

great sin. In his fulness of all kinds of intellectual gifts, he quite forgets from Whom he has his many gifts, and why it is that his despised neighbour has so few gifts. If you have ten or twenty talents, and I have only two, who is to be praised and who is to be blamed for that allotment? Your cleverness has misled you and has hitherto done you far more evil than good. You bear yourself among ordinary men, among less men than yourself, as if you had added all these cubits to your own stature. You ride over us as if you had already given in your account, and had heard it said, Take the one talent from them and give it to this my ten-talented servant. You seem to have set it down to your side of the great account, that you had such a good start in talent, and that your fine mind had so many tutors and governors all devoting themselves to your advancement. And you conduct yourself to us as if the Righteous Judge had cast us away from His presence, because we were not found among the wise and mighty of this world. The truth is, that the whole world is on a wholly wrong tack in its praise and in its blame. We praise the man of great gifts, and we blame the man of small gifts, completely forgetful that in so doing we give men the praise that belongs to God, and lay on men the blame, which, if there is any blame in the matter, ought to be laid elsewhere. Learn and lay to heart, my richly-gifted brethren, to be patient with all men, but especially to be patient with all stupid, slow-witted, ungifted, God-impoverished men. Do not add your insults and your ill-usage to the low estate of those on whom, in the meantime, God's hand lies so cold and so straitened. For who maketh thee to differ from another? and what hast thou that thou didst not receive? Now, if thou didst receive it, why dost thou glory as if thou hadst not received it? Call that to mind the next time you are tempted to cry out that you have no patience with your slow-witted servant.

3. 'Is patient with the bad' is one of the tributes of praise that is paid in the fine paraphrase to that heart that is full of the same love that is in God. A patient love to the unjust and the evil is one of the attributes and manifestations of the divine nature, as that nature is seen both in God and in all genuinely godly men. And, indeed, in no other thing is the divine nature so surely seen in any man as just in his love to and his patience with bad men. He schools and exercises himself every day to be patient and good to other men as God has been to him. He remembers when tempted to resentment how God did not resent his evil, but, while he was yet an enemy to God and to godliness, reconciled him to Himself by the death of His Son. And ever since the godly man saw that, he has tried to reconcile his worst enemies to himself by the death of his impatience and passion toward them, and has more pitied than blamed them, even when their evil was done against himself. Let God judge, and, if it must be, condemn that bad man. But I am too bad myself to cast a stone at the worst and most injurious of men. If we so much pity ourselves for our sinful lot, if we have so much compassion on ourselves because of our inherited and unavoidable estate of sin and misery, why do we not share our

pity and our compassion with those miserable men who are in an even worse estate than our own? At any rate, I must not judge them lest I be judged. I must take care when I say, Forgive me my trespasses, as I forgive them that trespass against me. Not to seven times must I grudgingly forgive, but ungrudgingly to seventy times seven. For with what judgment I judge, I shall be judged; and with what measure I mete, it shall be measured to me again.

> ' Love harbours no suspicious thought,
>   Is patient to the bad :
> Grieved when she hears of sins and crimes,
>   And in the truth is glad.'

4. And then, most difficult and most dangerous, but most necessary of all patience, we must learn how to be patient with ourselves. Every day we hear of miserable men rushing upon death because they can no longer endure themselves and the things they have brought on themselves. And there are moral suicides who cast off the faith and the hope and the endurance of a Christian man because they are so evil and have lived such an evil life. We speak of patience with bad men, but there is no man so bad, there is no man among all our enemies who has at all hurt us like that man who is within ourselves. And to bear patiently what we have brought upon ourselves,—to endure the inward shame, the self-reproof, the self-contempt bitterer to drink than blood, the lifelong injuries, impoverishment, and disgrace,—to bear all these patiently and uncomplainingly,—to acquiesce humbly in the discovery that all this was always in our hearts, and still is in our hearts—what humility,

what patience, what compassion and pity for ourselves must all that call forth! The wise nurse is patient with her passionate, greedy, untidy, disobedient child. She does not cast it out of doors, she does not run and leave it, she does not kill it because all these things have been and still are in its sad little heart. Her power for good with such a child lies just in her pity, in her compassion, and in her patience with her child. And the child that is in all of us is to be treated in the same patient, hopeful, believing, forgiving, divine way. We should all be with ourselves as God is with us. He knoweth our frame. He remembereth that we are dust. He shows all patience toward us. He does not look for great things from us. He does not break the bruised reed, nor quench the smoking flax. He shall not fail nor be discouraged till He have set judgment in the earth. And so shall not we.

5. And, then,—it is a sufficiently startling thing to say, but—we must learn to be patient with God also. All our patience, and all the exercises of it, if we think aright about it, all run up in the long-run into patience with God. But there are some exercises of patience that have to do directly and immediately with God and with God alone. When any man's heart has become fully alive to God and to the things of God; when he begins to see and feel that he lives and moves and has his being in God; then everything that in any way affects him is looked on by him as come to him from God. Absolutely, all things. The very weather that everybody is so atheistic about, the climate, the soil he labours, the

rain, the winter's cold and the summer's heat,—true piety sees all these things as God's things, and sees God's immediate will in the disposition and dispensation of them all. He feels the untameableness of his tongue in the indecent talk that goes on everlastingly about the weather. All these things may be without God to other men, as they once were to him also, but you will find that the truly and the intelligently devout man no longer allows himself in such unbecoming speech. For, though he cannot trace God's hand in all the changes of the seasons, in heat and cold, in sunshine and snow, yet he is as sure that God's wisdom and will are there as that Scripture is true and the Scripture-taught heart. 'Great is our Lord, and His understanding is infinite. Who covereth the heavens with clouds, and prepareth rain for the earth, and maketh the grass to grow upon the mountains. He giveth snow like wool; He scattereth the hoar-frost like ashes; He casteth forth His ice like morsels. Who can stand before his cold?' Here is the patience and the faith of the saints. Here are they that keep the commandments of God and the faith of Jesus Christ.

And, then, when through rain or frost or fire, when out of any terror by night or arrow that flieth by day, any calamity comes on the man who is thus pointed and practised in his patience, he is able with Job to say, 'This is the Lord. What, shall we receive good at the hand of God and not also receive evil?' By far the best thing I have ever read on this subject, and I have read it a thousand times since I first read it as a student, is Dr. Thomas Goodwin's *Patience and its Perfect Work*. That noble treatise had its origin in the great fire of London in 1666. The learned President of Magdalen College lost the half of his library, five hundred pounds worth of the best books, in that terrible fire. And his son tells us he had often heard his father say that in the loss of his not-to-be-replaced books, God had struck him in a very sensible place. To lose his Augustine, and his Calvin, and his Musculus, and his Zanchius, and his Amesius, and his Suarez, and his Estius was a sore stroke to such a man. I loved my books too well, said the great preacher, and God rebuked me by this affliction. Let the students here read Goodwin's costly treatise, and they will be the better prepared to meet such calamities as the burning of their manse and their library, as also to counsel and comfort their people when they shall lose their shops or their stackyards by fire.

> ' Blind unbelief is sure to err,
>   And scan His work in vain ;
>   God is His own interpreter,
>   And He will make it plain.'

And, then, in a multitude of New Testament scriptures, we are summoned to great exercise of patience with the God of our salvation, because it is His purpose and plan that we shall have to wait long for our salvation. God has not seen it good to carry us to heaven on the day of our conversion. He does not glorify us on the same day that He justifies us. We are appointed to salvation indeed, but it is also appointed us to wait long for it. This is not our rest. We are called to be pilgrims and strangers for a season with God upon the earth.

We are told to endure to the end. It is to be through faith and patience that we, with our fathers, shall at last inherit the promises. Holiness is not a Jonah's gourd. It does not come up in a night, and it does not perish in a night. Holiness is the Divine nature, and it takes a lifetime to make us partakers of it. But, then, if the time is long the thing is sure. Let us, then, with a holy and a submissive patience wait for it.

'I saw moreover in my dream that Passion seemed to be much discontent, but Patience was very quiet. Then Christian asked, What is the reason of the discontent of Passion? The Interpreter answered, The governor of them would have him stay for his best things till the beginning of the next year; but he will have them all now. But Patience is willing to wait.'

XI

SIMPLE, SLOTH, AND PRESUMPTION

'Ye did run well, who did hinder you?'—Paul.

T startles us not a little to come suddenly upon three pilgrims fast asleep with fetters on their heels on the upward side of the Interpreter's House, and even on the upward side of the cross and the sepulchre. We would have looked for those three miserable men somewhere in the City of Destruction or in the Town of Stupidity, or, at best, somewhere still outside of the wicket-gate. But John Bunyan did not lay down his *Pilgrim's Progress* on any abstract theory, or on any easy and pleasant presupposition, of the Christian life. He constructed his so lifelike book out of his own experiences as a Christian man, as well as out of all he had learned as a Christian minister. And in nothing is Bunyan's power of observation, deep insight, and firm hold of fact better seen than just in the way he names and places the various people of the pilgrimage. Long after he had been at the Cross of Christ himself, and had seen with his own eyes all the significant rooms in the Interpreter's House, Bunyan had often to confess that the fetters of evil habit, unholy affection, and a hard heart were still firmly riveted on his own heels.

And his pastoral work had led him to see only too
well that he was not alone in the temptations and
the dangers and the still-abiding bondage to sin
that had so surprised himself after he was so far on
in the Christian life. It was the greatest sorrow
of his heart, he tells us in a powerful passage in
his *Grace Abounding*, that so many of his spiritual
children broke down and came short in the arduous
and perilous way in which he had so hopefully
started them. 'If any of those who were awakened
by my ministry did after that fall back, as sometimes too many did, I can truly say that their loss
hath been more to me than if one of my own
children, begotten of my body, had been going to
its grave. I think, verily, I may speak it without
an offence to the Lord, nothing hath gone so near
me as that, unless it was the fear of the salvation of
my own soul. I have counted as if I had goodly
buildings and lordships in those places where my
children were born; my heart has been so wrapped
up in this excellent work that I counted myself
more blessed and honoured of God by this than if
He had made me the emperor of the Christian
world, or the lord of all the glory of the earth
without it.' And I have no doubt that we have
here the three things that above everything else
bereft Bunyan of so many of his spiritual children
personified and then laid down by the heels in
Simple, Sloth, and Presumption.

SIMPLE

Let us shake up Simple first and ask him what it
was that laid him so soon and in such a plight and

in such company in this bottom. It was not that which from his name we might at first think it was. It was not the weakness of his intellects, nor his youth, nor his inexperience. There is danger enough, no doubt, in all these things if they are not carefully attended to, but none of all these things in themselves, nor all of them taken together, will lay any pilgrim by the heels. There must be more than mere and pure simplicity. No blame attaches to a simple mind, much less to an artless and an open heart. We do not blame such a man even when we pity him. We take him, if he will let us, under our care, or we put him under better care, but we do not anticipate any immediate ill to him so long as he remains simple in mind, untainted in heart, and willing to learn. But, then, unless he is better watched over than any young man or young woman can well be in this world, that simplicity and child-likeness and inexperience of his may soon become a fatal snare to him. There is so much that is not simple and sincere in this world; there is so much false-hood and duplicity; there are so many men abroad whose endeavour is to waylay, mislead, entrap, and corrupt the simple-minded and the inexperienced, that it is next to impossible that any youth or maiden shall long remain in this world both simple and safe also. My son, says the Wise Man, keep my words, and lay up my commandments with thee. For at the window of my house I looked through my case-ment, and beheld among the simple ones, I discerned among the youths, a young man void of understand-ing;—and so on,—till a dart strike through his liver, and he goeth as an ox to the slaughter. And so, too often in our own land, the maiden in her simplicity also opens her ear to the promises and vows and oaths of the flatterer, till she loses both her simplicity and her soul, and lies buried in that same bottom beside Sloth and Presumption.

It is not so much his small mind and his weak understanding that is the fatal danger of their possessor, it is his imbecile way of treating his small mind. In our experience of him we cannot get him, all we can do, to read an instructive book. We cannot get him to attend our young men's class with all the baits and traps we can set for him. Where does he spend his Sabbath-day and week-day evenings? We cannot find out until we hear some distressing thing about him, that, ten to one, he would have escaped had he been a reader of good books, or a student with us, say, of Dante and Bunyan and Rutherford, and a companion of those young men and young women who talk about and follow such intellectual tastes and pursuits. Now, if you are such a young man or young woman as that, or such an old man or old woman, you will not be able to understand what in the world Bunyan can mean by saying that he saw you in his dream fast asleep in a bottom with irons on your heels. No; for to understand the *Pilgrim's Progress*, beyond a nursery and five-year-old understanding of it, you must have worked and studied and suffered your way out of your mental and spiritual imbecility. You must have for years attended to what is taught from the pulpit and the desk, and, alongside of that, you must have made a sobering and solemnising application of it all to your own heart. And then you would have seen and felt that the heels of your mind and of your heart are only too firmly fettered with the irons of ignorance and inexperience and self-complacency. But as it is, if you would tell the truth, you would say to us what Simple said to Christian, I see no danger. The next time that John Bunyan passed that bottom, the chains had been taken off the heels of this sleeping fool and had been put round his neck.

Sloth

Sloth had a far better head than Simple had; but what of that when he made no better use of it? There are many able men who lie all their days in a sad bottom with the irons of indolence and inefficiency on their heels. We often envy them their abilities, and say about them, What might they not have done for themselves and for us had they only worked hard? Just as we are surprised to see other men away above us on the mountain top, not because they have better abilities than we have, but because they tore the fetters of sloth out of their soft flesh and set themselves down doggedly to their work. And the same sloth that starves and fetters the mind at the same time casts the conscience and the heart into a deep sleep. I often wonder as I go on working among you, if you ever attach any meaning or make any application to yourselves of all those commands and counsels of which the Scriptures are full,—to be up and doing, to watch and pray, to watch and be sober, to fight the good fight of faith, to hold the fort, to rise early, and even by night, and to endure unto death, and never for one moment to be found off your guard. Do you attach any real meaning to these examples of the psalmists, to these continual commands and examples of Christ, and to these urgent counsels of His apostles? Do you? Against whom and against what do you thus campaign and fight? For fear of whom or of what do you thus watch? What fort do you hold? What occupies your thoughts in night-watches, and what inspires and compels your early prayers? It is your stupefying life of spiritual sloth that makes it impossible for you to answer these simple and superficial questions. Sloth is not the word for it. Let them give the right word to insanity like that who sleep and soak in sinful sloth no longer.

We have all enemies in our own souls that never sleep, whatever we may do. There are no irons on their heels. They never procrastinate. They never say to their master, A little more slumber. Now, could you name any hateful enemy entrenched in your own heart, of which you have of yourself said far more than that? And, if so, what have you done, what are you at this moment doing, to cast that enemy out? Have you any armour on, any weapons of offence and precision, against that enemy? And what success and what defeat have you had in unearthing and casting out that enemy? What fort do you hold? On what virtue, on what grace are you posted by your Lord to keep for yourself and for Him? And with what cost of meat and drink and sleep and amusement do you lose it or keep it for Him? Alexander used to leave his tent at midnight and go round the camp, and spear to his post the sentinel he found sleeping.

There is nothing we are all so slothful in as secret, particular, importunate prayer. We have an almighty instrument in our hand in secret and exact prayer if we would only importunately and perseveringly employ it. But there is an utterly unaccountable restraint of secret and particularising prayer in all of us. There is a soaking, stupefying sloth, that so fills our hearts that we forget and neglect the immense concession and privilege we have afforded us in secret prayer. Our sloth and stupidity in prayer is surely the last proof of our fall and of the misery of our fallen state. Our sloth with a gold mine open at our feet; a little more sleep on the top of a mast with a gulf under us that hath no bottom,—no language of this life can adequately describe the besottedness of that man who lies with irons on his heels between Simple and Presumption.

PRESUMPTION

The greatest theologian of the Roman Catholic Church has made an induction and classification of sins that has often been borrowed by our Protestant and Puritan divines. His classification is made, as will be seen, on an ascending scale of guilt and aggravation. In the world of sin, he says, there are, first, sins of ignorance; next, there are sins of infirmity; and then, at the top, there are sins of presumption. And this, it will be remembered, was the Psalmist's inventory and estimate of sins also. His last and his most earnest prayer was, that he might be kept back from all presumptuous sin. Now you know quite well, without any explanation, what presumption is. Don't presume, you say, with rising and scarce controlled anger. Don't presume too far. Take care, you say, with your heart beating so high that you can scarcely command it, take care lest you go too far. And the word of God feels and speaks about presumptuous sin very much as you do yourself.

Now, what gave this third man who lay in fetters a little beyond the cross the name of Presumption was just this, that he had been at the cross with his past sin, and had left the cross to commit the same sin at the first opportunity. Presumption presumed upon his pardon. He presumed upon the abounding grace of God. He presumed upon the blood of Christ. He was so high on the Atonement, that he held that the gospel was not sufficiently preached to him, unless not past sin only and present, but also all future sin was atoned for on the tree before it was committed. There is a reprobate in Dante, who, all the time he was repenting, had his eye on his next opportunity. Now, our Presumption was like that. He presumed on his youth, on his temptations, on his opportunities, and especially on his future reformation and the permanence and the freeness of the gospel offer. When he was in the Interpreter's House he did not hear what the Interpreter was saying, the blood was roaring so through his veins. His eyes were so full of other images that he did not see the man in the iron cage, nor the spider on the wall, nor the fire fed secretly. He had no more intention of keeping always to the way that was as straight as a rule could make it, than he had of cutting off both his hands and plucking out both his eyes. When the three shining ones stripped him of his rags and clothed him with change of raiment, he had no more intention of keeping his garments clean than he had of flying straight up to heaven on the spot. Now, let each man name to himself what that is in which he intentionally, deliberately, and by foresight and forethought sins. Have you named it? Well, it was for that that this reprobate was laid by the heels on the immediately hither side of the cross and the sepulchre. Not that the iron might not have been taken off his heels again on certain conditions, even after it was on; but, even so, he would never have been the same man again that he was before his presumptuous sin. You will easily know a man who has committed much presumptuous sin,—that is to say, if you have any eye for a sinner. I think I would find him out if I heard him pray once, or preach once, or even select a psalm for public or for family worship; even if I heard him say grace at a dinner-table, or reprove his son, or scold his servant. Presumptuous sin has so much of the venom and essence of sin in it that, forgiven or unforgiven, even a little of it never leaves the sinner as it found him. Even if his fetters are knocked off, there is always a piece of the poisonous iron left in his flesh; there is always a fang of his fetters left in the broken bone. The presumptuous saint will always be detected by the way he halts on his heels all his after days. Keep back Thy servant, O God, from presumptuous sin. Let him be innocent of the great transgression.

Dr. Thomas Goodwin says somewhere that the worm that dieth not only comes to its sharpest sting and to its deadliest venom when it is hatched up under gospel light. The very light of nature itself greatly aggravates some of our sins. The light of our early education greatly aggravates others of our sins. But nothing wounds our conscience and then exasperates the wound like a past experience of the same sin, and, especially, an experience of the grace of God in forgiving that sin. Had we found young Presumption in his irons before his conversion, we would have been afraid enough at the sight. Had we found him laid by the heels after his first uncleanness, it would have made us shudder for ourselves. But we are horrified and speechless as we see him apprehended and laid in irons on the very night of his first communion, and with the wine scarcely dry on his unclean lips. Augustine postponed his baptism till he should have his fill of sin, and till he should no longer return to sin like a dog to his vomit. Now, next Sabbath is our communion day in this congregation. Let us therefore this week examine ourselves. And if we must sin as long as we are in this world, let it henceforth be the sin of ignorance and of infirmity.

So the three reprobates lay down to sleep again, and Christian as he left that bottom went on in the narrow way singing:

> ' O to grace how great a debtor
>   Daily I 'm constrained to be ;
> Let that grace, Lord, like a fetter,
>   Bind my wandering heart to Thee.'

XII

THE THREE SHINING ONES AT THE CROSS

'Salvation shall God appoint for walls.'—*Isaiah*.

JOHN BUNYAN'S autobiography, *Grace Abounding to the Chief of Sinners*, is the best of all our commentaries on *The Pilgrim's Progress*, and again to-night I shall have to fall back on that incomparable book. 'Now, I saw in my dream that the highway up which Christian was to go was fenced on either side with a wall, and that wall is called Salvation. Up this way, therefore, did burdened Christian run, but not without great difficulty, because of the load on his back.' In the corresponding paragraph in *Grace Abounding*, our author says, speaking about himself: 'But forasmuch as the passage was wonderful narrow, even so narrow that I could not but with great difficulty enter in thereat, it showed me that none could enter into life but those that were in downright earnest, and unless also they left this wicked world behind them; for here was only room for body and soul, but not for body and soul and sin.' 'He ran thus till he came to a place somewhat ascending, and upon that place stood a cross, and a little below in the bottom a sepulchre. So I saw in my dream, that just as Christian came up with this cross, his burden loosed from off his shoulders and fell from off his back, and began to tumble, and so continued to do till it came to the mouth of the sepulchre, where it fell in, and I saw it no more.' Turning again to the *Grace Abounding*, we read in the 115th paragraph: 'I remember that one day as I was travelling into the country and musing on the wickedness and blasphemy of my heart, and considering of the enmity that was in me to God, that scripture came into my mind, He hath made peace by the blood of His Cross. By which I was made to see both again and again and again that day that God and my soul were friends by that blood : yea, I saw that the justice of God and my sinful soul could embrace and kiss each other through that blood. That was a good day to me ; I hope I shall not forget it. I thought I could have spoken of His love and of His mercy to me that day to the very crows that sat upon the ploughed lands before me had they been capable to have understood me. Wherefore I said in my soul with much gladness, Well, I would I had a pen and ink here and I would write this down before I go any farther, for surely I will not forget this forty years hence.'

From all this we learn that the way to the Celestial City lies within high and close fencing walls. There is not room for many pilgrims to walk abreast in that way ; indeed, there is seldom room for two. There are some parts of the way where two or even three pilgrims can for a time walk and converse together, but for the most part the path is distressingly lonely. The way is so fenced up also that a pilgrim cannot so much as look either to the right hand or the left. Indeed, it is one of the laws of that road that no man is to attempt to look except straight on before him. But then there is this compensation for the solitude and stringency of the way that the wall that so encloses it is Salvation. And Salvation is such a wall that it is companionship and prospect enough of itself. Dante saw a long reach of this same wall running round the bottom of the mount that cleanses him who climbs it,—a long stretch of such sculptured beauty, that it arrested him and instructed him and delighted him beyond his power sufficiently to praise it. And thus, that being so, burdened and bowed down to the earth as our pilgrim was, he was on the sure way, sooner or later, to deliverance. Somewhere and sometime and somehow on that steep and high fenced way deliverance was sure to come. And, then, as to the burdened man himself. His name was once Graceless, but his name is Graceless no longer. No graceless man runs long between these close and cramping-up walls; and, especially, no graceless man has that burden long on his back. That is not Graceless any longer who is leaving the Interpreter's House for the fenced way; that is Christian, and as long as he remains Christian, the closeness of the fence and the weight of his burden are a small matter. But long-looked-for comes at last. And so, still carrying his burden and keeping close within the fenced-up way, our pilgrim came at last to a cross. And a perfect miracle immediately took place in that somewhat ascending ground. For scarcely had Christian set his eyes on the cross, when, without his pulling at it, or pushing it, or even at that moment thinking of it, ere ever he was aware, he saw his burden begin to tumble, and so it continued to do till it fell fairly out of his sight into an open sepulchre.

The application of all that is surely self-evident. For our way in a holy life is always closely fenced up. It is far oftener a lonely way than otherwise. And the steepness, sternness, and loneliness of our way are all aggravated by the remembrance of our past sins and follies. They still, and more and more, lie upon our hearts a heart-crushing burden. But if we, like Christian, know how to keep our back to our former house and our face to heaven, sooner or later we too shall surely come to the cross. And then, either suddenly, or after a long agony, our burden also shall be taken off our back and shut down into Christ's sepulchre. And I saw it no more, says the dreamer. He does not say that its owner saw it no more. He was too wise and too true a dreamer to say that.

It will be remembered that the first time we saw this man, with whose progress to the Celestial City we are at present occupied, he was standing in a certain place clothed with rags and with a burden on his back. After a long journey with him, we have just seen his burden taken off his back, and it is only after his burden is off and a Shining One has said to him, Thy sins be forgiven, that a second Shining One comes and strips him of his rags and clothes him with change of raiment. Now, why, it may be asked, has Christian had to carry his burden so long, and why is he still kept so ragged and so miserable and he so far on in the pilgrim's path?

Surely, it will be said, John Bunyan was dreaming indeed when he kept a truly converted man, a confessedly true and sincere Christian, so long in bonds and in rags. Well, as to his rags : filthy rags are only once spoken of in the Bible, and it is the prophet Isaiah, whose experience and whose language John Bunyan had so entirely by heart, who puts them on. And that evangelist among the prophets not only calls his own and Israel's sins filthy rags, but Isaiah is very bold, and calls their very righteousnesses by that opprobrious name. Had that bold prophet said that all his and all his people's *un*righteousnesses were filthy rags, all Israel would have subscribed to that. There was no man so brutish as not to admit that. But as long as they had any sense of truth and any self-respect, multitudes of Isaiah's first hearers and readers would resent what he so rudely said of their righteousnesses. On the other hand, the prophet's terrible discovery and comparison, just like our dreamer's dramatic distribution of Christian experience, was, to a certainty, an immense consolation to many men in Israel in his day. They gathered round Isaiah because, but for him and his evangelical ministry, they would have been alone in their despair. To them Isaiah's ministry was a house of refuge, and the prophet himself a veritable tower of strength. They felt they were not alone so long as Isaiah dwelt in the same city with them. And thus, whatever he might be to others, he was God's very prophet to them as his daily prayers in the temple both cast them down and lifted them up. 'Oh that Thou wouldst rend the heavens and come down. . . . But we are all as an unclean thing, and all our righteousnesses are as filthy rags, and our iniquities like the wind have taken us away.' Thousands in Israel found in these terrible words a door of hope, a sense of fellowship, and a call to trust and thanksgiving. And tens of thousands have found the same help and consolation out of what have seemed to others the very darkest and most perplexing pages of the *Pilgrim's Progress* and the *Grace Abounding*. 'It made me greatly ashamed,' says Hopeful, 'of the vileness of my former life, and confounded me with the sense of mine own ignorance, for there never came into mine heart before now that showed me so by contrast the beauty of the Lord Jesus. My own vileness and nakedness made me love a holy life. Yea, I thought that had I now a thousand gallons of blood in my body, I could spill it all for the sake of the Lord Jesus.' And if you, my brother, far on in the way of Salvation, still think sometimes that, after all, you must be a reprobate because of your filthy rags, read what David Brainerd wrote with his half-dead hand on the last page of his seraphic journal : 'How sweet it is to love God and to have a heart all for God ! Yes ; but a voice answered me, You are not all for God, you are not an angel. To which my whole soul replied, I as sincerely desire to love and glorify God as any angel in heaven. But you are filthy, and not fit for heaven. When hereupon there instantly appeared above me and spread over me the blessed robes of Christ's righteousness which I could not but exult and triumph in. And then I knew that I should be as active as an angel in heaven, and should then be for ever stripped of my filthy garments and clothed with spotless raiment.' Let me die the death of David Brainerd, and let my latter end be like his !

The third Shining One then came forward and set a mark on the forehead of this happy man. And it was a most ancient and a most honourable mark. For it was the same redeeming mark that was set by Moses upon the foreheads of the children of Israel when the Lord took them into covenant with Himself at the Passover in the wilderness. It was the same distinguishing mark also that the man with the slaughter-weapon in his hand first set upon the foreheads of the men who sighed and cried for the abominations that were done in the midst of Jerusalem. And it was the same glorious mark that John saw in the foreheads of the hundred and forty and four thousand who stood upon Mount Zion and sang a song that no man knew but those men who had been redeemed from the earth by the blood of the Lamb. The mark was set for propriety and for ornament and for beauty. It was set upon his forehead so that all who looked on him ever after might thus know to what company and what country he belonged, and that this was not his rest, but that he had been called and chosen to a heavenly inheritance. And, besides, it was no sooner set upon his forehead than it greatly added to his dignity and his comeliness. He had now the gravity and beauty of an angel ; nay, the beauty in his measure and the gravity of Goodwill at the gate himself. And, then, as if that were not enough, the third Shining One also gave him a roll with a seal upon it, which he was bidden look on as he ran, and which he was to give in when he arrived at the Celestial Gate. Now, what was that sealed roll but just the inward memory and record of all this pilgrim's experiences of the grace of God from the day he set out on pilgrimage down to that day when he stood un- burdened of his guilt, unclothed of his rags, and clothed upon with change of raiment ? The roll con- tained his own secret life, all sealed and shone in upon by the light of God's countenance. The secret of the Lord with this pilgrim was written within that roll, a secret that no man could read but he himself alone. It was the same roll that this same Shining One gave to Abraham, the first pilgrim and the father of all true pilgrims, after Melchizedek, the priest of the Most High God, had brought forth bread and wine and had blessed that great believer 'Fear not, Abram : I am thy shield, and thy exceeding great reward.' And, again, after Abram had lost his roll, like our pilgrim in the arbour, when he re- covered it he read thus in it : 'I am the Almighty God : walk before Me, and be thou perfect. And I will make My covenant between Me and thee.' And Abram fell on his face for joy. It was the same roll out of which the Psalmist proposed to read a passage to all those in his day who feared God. 'Come and hear, all ye that fear God, and I will declare what He hath done for my soul.' It was the same roll also that God sent to Israel in his sore captivity. 'Fear not, O Israel, for I have re- deemed thee ; I have called thee by thy name, thou art Mine. When thou passest through the waters, I will be with thee.' The high priest Joshua also had the same roll put into his hand, and that not only for his own comfort, but to make him the comforter of God's afflicted people. For after the Lord had plucked Joshua as a brand out of the fire, and had made his iniquity to pass from him, and had clothed him with change of raiment, and had set a fair mitre on his head, the Lord gave to Joshua a sealed roll, the contents of which may be read to this day in the book of the prophet Zechariah. Nay, more: 'Will you have me to speak plainly?' says great Goodwin on this matter. 'Then, though our Lord had the assurance of faith that He was the Son of God, for He knew it out of the Scriptures by reading all the prophets, yet, to have it sealed to Him with joy unspeakable and glorious,—this was deferred to the time of His baptism. He was then anointed with the oil of assurance and gladness in a more peculiar and transcendent manner.' 'In His baptism,' says Bengel, 'our Lord was magnificently enlightened. He was previously the Son of God, and yet the power of the Divine testimony to His Sonship at His baptism long affected Him in a lively manner.' And we see our Lord reading His roll to assure and sustain His heart when all outward acceptance and sustenance failed Him. 'There is One who beareth witness of Me, and His witness is true. I receive not witness from men. I have a greater witness than even that of John. For the Father Himself that hath sent Me, He beareth witness of Me.' No wonder that our heavy-laden pilgrim of yesterday gave three leaps for joy and went on singing with such a roll as that in his bosom. For, at that supreme moment he had that inward illumination and assurance sealed on his heart that had so gladdened and sustained so many prophets and psalmists and apostles and saints before his day. And though, like Abraham and all the other saints who ever had that noble roll put into their keeping, except Jesus Christ, he often lost it, yet as often as he again recovered it, it brought back again with it all his first joy and gladness.

But, as was said at the beginning, the *Grace Abounding* is the best of all our commentaries on *The Pilgrim's Progress.* As thus here also: 'Now had I an evidence, as I thought, of my salvation from heaven, with many golden seals thereon, all hanging in my sight. Now could I remember this manifestation and that other discovery of grace with comfort, and should often long and desire that the last day were come, that I might be for ever inflamed with the sight and joy of Him and communion with Him whose head was crowned with thorns, whose face was spit on, and body broken, and soul made an offering for my sins. For whereas, before, I lay continually trembling at the mouth of hell, now, methought, I was got so far therefrom that I could not, when I looked back, scarce discern it. And oh! thought I, that I were fourscore years old now, that I might die quickly, that my soul might be gone to rest.'

Then Christian gave three leaps for joy and went on singing:

'Thus far did I come laden with my sin,
Nor could ought ease the grief that I was in
Till I came hither: . . .
Blest Cross! blest Sepulchre! blest rather be
The Man that there was put to shame for me.'

XIII

FORMALIST AND HYPOCRISY

'A form of godliness.'—*Paul.*

E all began our religious life by being formalists. And we were not altogether to blame for that. Our parents were first to blame for that, and then our teachers, and then our ministers. They made us say our psalm and our catechism to them, and if we only said our sacred lesson without stumbling, we were straightway rewarded with their highest praise. They seldom took the trouble to make us understand the things we said to them. They were more than content with our correct repetition of the words. We were never taught either to read or repeat with our eyes on the object. And we had come to our manhood before we knew how to seek for the visual image that lies at the root of all our words. And thus the ill-taught schoolboy became in us the father of the confirmed formalist. The mischief of this neglect still spreads through the whole of our life, but it is absolutely disastrous in our religious life. Look at the religious formalist at family worship with his household gathered round him all in his own image. He would not on any account let his family break up any night without the habitual duty. He has a severe method in his religious duties that nothing is ever allowed to disarrange or in any way to interfere with. As the hour strikes, the big Bible is brought out. He opens where he left off last night, he reads the regulation chapter, he leads the singing in the regulation psalm, and then, as from a book, he repeats his regulation prayer. But he never says a word to show that he either sees or feels what he reads, and his household break up without an idea in their heads or an affection in their hearts. He comes to church and goes through public worship in the same wooden way, and he sits through the Lord's Table in the same formal and ceremonious manner. He has eyes of glass and hands of wood, and a heart without either blood or motion in it. His mind and his heart were destroyed in his youth, and all his religion is a religion of rites and ceremonies without sense or substance. 'Because I knew no better,' says Bunyan, 'I fell in very eagerly with the religion of the times : to wit, to go to church twice a day, and that, too, with the foremost. And there should I sing and say as others did. Withal, I was so overrun with the spirit of superstition that I adored, and that with great devotion, even all things, both the high place, priest, clerk, vestment, service, and what else belonged to the church : counting all things holy that were therein contained. But all this time I was not sensible of the danger and evil of sin. I was kept from considering that sin would damn me, what religion soever I followed, unless I was found in Christ. Nay, I never thought of Christ, nor whether there was one or no.'

A formalist is not yet a hypocrite exactly, but he is ready now and well on the way at any moment to become a hypocrite. As soon now as some temptation shall come to him to make appear another and a better man than he really is : when in some way it becomes his advantage to seem to other people to be a spiritual man : when he thinks he sees his way to some profit or praise by saying things and doing things that are not true and natural to him,—then he will pass on from being a bare and simple formalist, and will henceforth become a hypocrite. He has never had any real possession or experience of spiritual things amid all his formal observances of religious duties, and he has little or no difficulty, therefore, in adding another formality or two to his former life of unreality. And thus the transition is easily made from a comparatively innocent and unconscious formalist to a conscious and studied hypocrite. 'An hypocrite,' says Samuel Rutherford, 'is he who on the stage represents a king when he is none, a beggar, an old man, a husband, when he is really no such thing. To the Hebrews, they were *faciales*, face-men ; *colorati*, dyed men, red men, birds of many colours. You may paint a man, you may paint a rose, you may paint a fire burning, but you cannot paint a soul, or the smell of a rose, or the heat of a fire. And it is hard to counterfeit spiritual graces, such as love to Christ, sincere intending of the glory of God, and such like spiritual things.' Yes, indeed ; it is hard to put on and to go through with a truly spiritual grace even to the best and most spiritually-minded of men ; and as for the true hypocrite, he never honestly attempts it. If he ever did honestly and resolutely attempt it, he would at once in that pass out of the ranks of the hypocrites altogether and pass over into a very different category. Bunyan lets us see how a formalist and a hypocrite and a Christian all respectively do when they come to a real difficulty. The three pilgrims were all walking in the same path, and with their faces for the time in the same direction. They had not held much conference together since their first conversation, and as time goes on, Christian has no more talk but with himself, and that sometimes sighingly, and sometimes more comfortably. When, all at once, the three men come on the hill Difficulty. A severe act of self-denial has to be done at this point of their pilgrimage. A proud heart has to be humbled to the dust. A second, a third, a tenth place has to be taken in the praise of men. An outbreak of anger and wrath has to be kept under for hours and days. A great injury, a scandalous case of ingratitude, has to be forgiven and forgotten; in short, as Rutherford says, an impossible-to-be-counterfeited spiritual grace has to be put into its severest and sorest exercise; and the result was—what we know. Our pilgrim went and drank of the spring that always runs at the bottom of the hill Difficulty, and thus refreshed himself against that hill; while Formalist took the one low road, and Hypocrisy the other, which led him into a wide field full of dark mountains, where he stumbled and fell and rose no more. When, after his visit to the spring, Christian began to go up the hill, saying:

> ' This hill, though high, I covet to ascend ;
> The difficulty will not me offend ;
> For I perceive the way to life lies here ;
> Come, pluck up heart ; let 's neither faint nor fear ;
> Better, though difficult, the right way to go,
> Than wrong, though easy, where the end is woe.'

Now, all this brings us to the last step in the evolution of a perfect hypocrite out of a simple formalist. The perfect and finished hypocrite is not your commonplace and vulgar scoundrel of the playwright and the penny-novelist type ; the finest hypocrite is a character their art cannot touch. 'The worst of hypocrites,' Rutherford goes on to say, 'is he who whitens himself till he deceives himself. It is strange that a man hath such power over himself. But a man's heart may deceive his heart, and he may persuade himself that he is godly and righteous when he knows nothing about it.' 'Preaching in a certain place,' says Boston, 'after supper the mistress of the house told me how I had terrified God's people. This was by my doctrine of self-love, self-righteousness, self-ends, and such like. She restricted hypocrites to that sort that do all things to be seen of men, and harped much on this —how can one be a hypocrite who hates hypocrisy in other people? how can one be a hypocrite and not know it ? All this led me to see the need of such doctrine.' And if only to show you that this is not the dismal doctrine of antediluvian Presbyterians only, Canon Mozley says : 'The Pharisee did not know that he was a Pharisee ; if he had known it he would not have been a Pharisee. He does not know that he is a hypocrite. The vulgar hypocrite knows that he is a hypocrite because he deceives others, but the true Scripture hypocrite deceives himself.' And the most subtle teacher of our century, or of any century, has said: 'What is a hypocrite? We are apt to understand by a hypocrite one who makes a profession of religion for secret ends, without practising what he professes; who is malevolent, covetous, or profligate, while he assumes an outward sanctity in his words and conduct, and who does so deliberately, deceiving others, and not at all self-deceived. But this is not what our Saviour seems to have meant by a hypocrite; nor were the Pharisees such. The Pharisees deceived themselves as well as others. Indeed, it is not in human nature to deceive others for any long time without in a measure deceiving ourselves also. When they began, each in his turn, to deceive the people, they were not at the moment self-deceived. But by degrees they forgot that outward ceremonies avail nothing without inward purity. They did not know themselves, and they unawares deceived themselves as well as the people.' What a terrible light, as of the last day itself, does all that cast upon the formalisms and the hypocrisies of which our own religious life is full! And what a terrible light it casts on those miserable men who are complete and finished in their self-deception! For the complete and finished hypocrite is not he who thinks that he is better than all other men; that is hopeless enough; but the paragon of hypocrisy is he who does not know that he is worse than all other men. And in his stone-blindness to himself, and consequently to all reality and inwardness and spirituality in religion, you see him intensely interested in, and day and night occupied with, the outside things of religion, till nothing short of a miracle will open his eyes. See him in the ministry, for instance, sweating at his sermons and in his visiting, till you would almost think that he is the minister of whom Paul prophesied, who should spend and be spent for the salvation of men's souls. But all the time, such is the hypocrisy that haunts the ministerial calling, he is really and at bottom animated with ambition for the praise of men only, and for the increase of his congregation. See him, again, now assailing or now defending a church's secular privileges, and he knowing no more, all the time, what a church has been set up for on earth than the man in the moon. What a penalty his defence is and his support to a church of Christ, and what an incubus his membership must be ! Or, see him, again, making long speeches and many prayers for the extension of the kingdom of Christ, and all the time spending ten times more on wine or whisky or tobacco, or on books or pictures or foreign travel, than he gives to the cause of home or foreign missions. And so on, all through our hypocritical and self-blinded life. Through such stages, and to such a finish, does the formalist pass from his thoughtless and neglected youth to his hardened, blinded, self-seeking life, spent in the ostensible service of the church of Christ. If the light that is in such men be darkness, how great is that darkness ! We may all well shudder as we hear our Lord saying to ministers and members and church defenders and church supporters like ourselves : 'Now ye say, We see ; therefore your sin remaineth.'

Now, the first step to the cure of all such hypo-crisy, and to the salvation of our souls, is to know that we are hypocrites, and to know also what that is in which we are most hypocritical. Well, there are two absolutely infallible tests of a true hypo-crite,—tests warranted to unmask, expose, and condemn the most finished, refined, and even evangelical hypocrite in this house to-night, or in all the world. By far and away the best and swiftest is prayer. True prayer, that is. For here again our inexpugnable hypocrisy comes in and leads us down to perdition even in our prayers. There is nothing our Lord more bitterly and more con-temptuously assails the Pharisees for than just the length, the loudness, the number, and the publicity of their prayers. The truth is, public prayer, for the most part, is no true prayer at all. It is at best an open homage paid to secret prayer. We make such shipwrecks of devotion in public prayer, that if we have a shred of true religion about us, we are glad to get home and to shut our door. We preach in our public prayers. We make speeches on public men and on public events in our public prayers. We see the reporters all the time in our public prayers. We do everything but pray in our public prayers. And to get away alone,—what an escape that is from the temptations and defeats of public prayer! No; public prayer is no test whatever of a hypocrite. A hypocrite revels in public prayer. It is secret prayer that finds him out. And even secret prayer will sometimes deceive us. We are crushed down on our secret knees sometimes, by sheer shame and the strength of conscience. Fear of exposure, fear of death and hell, will sometimes make us shut our door. A flood of passing feeling will sometimes make us pray for a season in secret. Job had all that before him when he said, 'Will the hypocrite delight himself in the Almighty? will he always call upon God?' No, he will not. And it is just here that the hypocrite and the true Christian best discover themselves both to God and to themselves. The true Christian will, as Job again says, pray in secret till God slays him. He will pray in his dreams; he will pray till death; he will pray after he is dead. Are you in earnest, then, not to be any more a hypocrite and to know the infallible marks of such? Ask the key of your closet door. Ask the chair at your bedside. Ask the watchman what you were doing and why your light was in so long. Ask the birds of the air and the beasts of the field and the crows on the ploughed lands after your solitary walk.

Almost a better test of true and false religion than even secret prayer, but a test that is far more difficult to handle, is our opinion of ourselves. In His last analysis of the truly justified man and the truly reprobate, our Lord made the deepest test to be their opinion of themselves. 'God, I thank Thee that I am not as this publican,' said the hypocrite. 'God be merciful to me a sinner,' said the true penitent. And then this fine principle comes in here —not only to speed the sure sanctification of a true Christian, but also, if he has skill and courage to use it, for his assurance and comfort,—that the saintlier he becomes and the riper for glory, the more he will beat his breast over what yet abides within his breast. Yes; a man's secret opinion of himself is almost a better test of his true spiritual state than even secret prayer. But, then, these two are not competing and exclusive tests; they always go together and are never found apart. And at the mouth of these two witnesses every true hypocrite shall be condemned and every true Christian justified.

Dr. Pusey says somewhere that the perfect hypocrite is the man who has the truth of God in his mind, but is without the love of God in his heart. 'Truth without love,' says that saintly scholar, 'makes a finished Pharisee.' Now, we Scottish and Free Church people believe we have the truth, if any people on the face of the earth have it; and if we have not love mixed with it, you see where and what we are. We are called to display a banner because of the truth, but let love always be our flag-staff. Let us be jealous for the truth, but let it be a godly, that is to say, a loving jealousy. When we contend for purity of doctrine and for purity of worship, when we protest against popery and priest-craft, when we resist rationalism and infidelity, when we do battle now for national religion, as we call it, and now for the freedom of the church, let us do it all in love to all men, else we had better not do it at all. If we cannot do it with clean and all-men-loving hearts, let us leave all debate and contention to stronger and better men than we are. The truth will never be advanced or guarded by us, nor will the Lord of truth and love accept our service or bless our souls, till we put on the divine nature, and have our hearts and our mouths still more full of love than our minds and our mouths are full of truth. Let us watch ourselves, lest with all our so-called love of truth we be found reprobates at last ; because we loved the truth for some selfish or party end, and hated and despised our brother, and believed all evil and disbelieved all good concerning our brother. Truth without love makes a hypocrite, says Dr. Pusey; and evangelical truth without evangelical love makes an evangelical hypocrite, says Thomas Shepard. Only where the whole truth is united to a heart full of love have we the perfect New Testament Christian.

XIV

TIMOROUS AND MISTRUST

'There is a lion in the way.'—*The Slothful Man.*
'I must venture.'—*Christian.*

 AT any rate must venture,' said Christian to Timorous and Mistrust· 'Whatever you may do I must venture, even if the lions you speak of should pull me to pieces. I, for one, shall never go back. To go back is nothing but death ; to go forward is fear of death and ever-lasting life beyond it. I will yet go forward.' So Mistrust and Timorous ran down the hill, and Christian went on his way. George Offor says, in his notes on this passage, that civil despotism and ecclesiastical tyranny so terrified many young converts in John Bunyan's day, that multitudes turned back like Mistrust and Timorous ; while at the same time, many like Bunyan himself went forward and for a time fell into the lion's mouth. Civil despotism and ecclesiastial tyranny do not stand in our way as they stood in Bunyan's way—at least, not in the same shape : but every age has its own lions, and every Christian man has his own lions that neither civil despots nor ecclesiastical tyrants know anything about.

Now, who or what is the lion in your way ? Who

or what is it that fills you with such timorousness
and mistrust, that you are almost turning back from
the way to life altogether? The fiercest of all our
lions is our own sin. When a man's own sin not
only finds him out and comes roaring after him, but
when it dashes past him and gets into the woods
and thickets before him, and stands pawing and
foaming on the side of his way, that is a trial of faith
and love and trust indeed. Sometimes a man's
past sins will fill all his future life with sleepless
apprehensions. He is never sure at what turn in
his upward way he may not suddenly run against
some of them standing ready to rush out upon him.
And it needs no little quiet trust and humble-
minded resignation to carry a man through this
slough and that bottom, up this hill and down that
valley, all the time with his life in his hand; and
yet at every turn, at every rumour that there are
lions in the way, to say, Come lion, come lamb,
come death, come life, I must venture, I will yet go
forward. As Job also, that wonderful saint of God,
said, 'Hold your peace, let me alone that I may
speak, and let come on me what will. Wherefore do
I take my flesh in my teeth and put my life in my
hand? Though He slay me, yet will I trust in
Him. He also shall be my salvation; for an
hypocrite shall not come before Him.'

One false step, one stumble in life, one error in
judgment, one outbreak of an unbridled temperament, one small sin, if it is even so much as a sin,
of ignorance or of infirmity, will sometimes not only
greatly injure us at the time, but, in some cases,
will fill all our future life with trials and difficulties

and dangers. Many of us shall have all our days to face a future of defeat, humiliation, impoverishment, and many hardships, that has not come on us on account of any presumptuous transgression of God's law so much as simply out of some combination of unfortunate circumstances in which we may have only done our duty, but have not done it in the most serpent-like way. And when we are made to suffer unjustly or disproportionately all our days for our error of judgment or our want of the wisdom of this world, or what not, we are sorely tempted to be bitter and proud and resentful and unforgiving, and to go back from duty and endurance and danger altogether. But we must not. We must rather say to ourselves, Now and here, if not in the past, I must play the man, and, by God's help, the wise man. I must pluck safety henceforth out of the heart of the nettle danger. Yes, I made a mistake. I did what I would not do now, and I must not be too proud to say so. I acted, I see now, precipitately, inconsiderately, imprudently. And I must not gloom and rebel and run away from the cross and the lion. I must not insist or expect that the always wise and prudent man's reward is to come to me. The lion in my way is a lion of my own rearing; and I must not turn my back on him, even if he should be let loose to leap on me and rend me. I must pass under his paw and through his teeth, if need be, to a life with him and beyond him of humility and duty and quiet-hearted submission to his God and mine.

Then, again, our salvation itself sometimes, our true sanctification, puts on a lion's skin and not

unsuccessfully imitates an angry lion's roar. Some
saving grace that up till now we have been fatally
lacking in lies under the very lip of that lion we see
standing straight in our way. God in His wisdom
so orders our salvation, that we must work out the
best part of it with fear and trembling. Right
before us, just beside us, standing over us with his
heavy paw upon us, is a lion, from under whose paw
and from between whose teeth we must pluck and
put on that grace in which our salvation lies. Repentance and reformation lie in the way of that lion;
resignation also and humility ; the crucifixion of our
own will ; the sacrifice of our own heart ; in short,
everything that is still lacking but is indispensable
to our salvation lies through that den of lions. One
man here is homeless and loveless ; another is child-
less ; another has a home and children, and much
envies the man who has neither ; one has talents
there is no scope for ; another has the scope, but
not the sufficient talent ; another must now spend
all his remaining life in a place where he sees that
anger and envy and jealousy and malevolence will
be his roaring lions daily seeking to devour his soul.
There is not a Christian man or woman in this house
whose salvation, worth being called a salvation, does
not lie through such a lion's thicket as that. Our
Lord Himself was a roaring lion to John the Baptist.
For the Baptist's salvation lay not in his powerful
preaching, but in his being laid aside from all
preaching ; not in his crowds increasing, but in his
Successor's crowds increasing and his decreasing.
The Baptist was the greatest born of woman in that
day, not because he was a thundering preacher—

any ordinary mother in Israel might have been his mother in that : but to decrease sweetly and to steal down quietly to perfect humility and self-oblivion,—that salvation was reserved for the son of Elisabeth alone. I would not like to say Who that is champing and pawing for your blood right in your present way. Reverence will not let me say Who it is. Only, you venture on Him.

'Yes, I shall venture!' said Christian to the two terrified and retreating men. Now, every true venture is made against risk and uncertainty, against anxiety and danger and fear. And it is just this that constitutes the nobleness and blessedness of faith. Faith sells all for Christ. Faith risks all for eternal life. Faith faces all for salvation. When it is at the worst, faith still says, Very well; even if there is no Celestial City anywhere in the world, it is better to die still seeking it than to live on in the City of Destruction. Even if there is no Jesus Christ,—I have read about Him and heard about Him and pictured Him to myself, till, say what you will, I shall die kissing and embracing that Divine Image I have in my heart. Even if there is neither mercy-seat nor intercession in heaven, I shall henceforth pray without ceasing. Far far better for me all the rest of my sinful life to be clothed with sackcloth and ashes, even if there is no fountain opened in Jerusalem for sin and uncleanness, and no change of raiment. Christian protested that, as for him, lions and all, he had no choice left. And no more have we. He must away somewhere, anywhere, from his past life. And so must we. If all the lions that ever drank blood are to collect upon his way, let them do so ; they shall not all make him turn back. Why should they ? What is a whole forest full of lions to a heart and a life full of sin? Lions are like lambs compared with sin. 'Good morning ! I for one must venture. I shall yet go forward.' So Mistrust and Timorous ran down the hill, and Christian went on his way.

So I saw in my dream that he made haste and went forward, that if possible he might get lodging in the house called Beautiful that stood by the highway side. Now, before he had gone far he entered into a very narrow passage which was about a furlong off from the porter's lodge, and looking very narrowly before him as he went, he espied two lions in the way. Then was he afraid, and thought also to go back, for he thought that nothing but death was before him. But the porter at the lodge, whose name was Watchful, perceiving that Christian made a halt, as if he would go back, cried unto him, saying, 'Is thy strength so small? Fear not the lions, for they are chained, and are only placed there for the trial of faith where it is, and for the discovery of those who have none. Keep the midst of the path and no hurt shall come to thee.' Yes, that is all we have to do. Whatever our past life may have been, whatever our past sins, past errors of judgment, past mistakes and mishaps, whatever of punishment or chastisement or correction or instruction or sanctification and growth in grace may be under those lions' skins and between their teeth for us, all we have got to do at present is to leave the lions to Him who set them there, and to go on, up to them and past them, keeping always to the midst of the path. The lions may roar at us till they have roared us deaf and blind, but we are far safer in the midst of that path than we would be in our own bed. Only let us keep in the midst of the path. When their breath is hot and full of blood on our cheek; when they paw up the blinding earth; when we feel as if their teeth had closed round our heart,—still, all the more, let us keep in the midst of the path. We must sometimes walk on a razor-edge of fear and straightforwardness; that is the only way left for us now. But, then, we have the Divine assurance that on that perilous edge no hurt shall come to us. 'Temptations,' says our author in another place, 'when we meet them at first, are as the lion that roared upon Samson; but if we overcome them, the next time we see them we shall find a nest of honey in them.' O God, for grace and sense and imagination to see and understand and apply all that to our own daily life! O to be able to take all that home to-night and see it all there; lions and runaways, venturesome souls, narrow paths, palaces of beauty, everlasting life and all! Open Thou our eyes that we may see the wonderful things that await us in our own house at home!

'Things out of hope are compassed oft with venturing.'

So they are; and so they were that day with our terrified pilgrim. He made a venture at the supreme moment of his danger, and things that were quite out of all hope but an hour before were then compassed and ever after possessed by him. Make the same venture, then, yourselves to-night.

Naught venture, naught have. Your lost soul is not much to venture, but it is all that Christ at this moment asks of you—that you leave your lost soul in His hand, and then go straight on from this moment in the middle of the path: the path, that is, as your case may be, of purity, humility, submission, resignation, and self-denial. Keep your mind and your heart, your eyes and your feet, in the very middle of that path, and you shall have compassed the House Beautiful before you know. The lions shall soon be behind you, and the grave and graceful damsels of the House—Discretion and Prudence and Piety and Charity — shall all be waiting upon you.

XV

PRUDENCE [1]

'Let a man examine himself.'—*Paul.*

LET a man examine himself, says the apostle to the Corinthians, and so let him eat of that bread and drink of that cup. And thus it was, that before the pilgrim was invited to sit down at the supper table in the House Beautiful, quite a number of most pointed and penetrating questions were put to him by those who had charge of that house and its supper table. And thus the time was excellently improved till the table was spread, while the short delay and the successive exercises whetted to an extraordinary sharpness the pilgrim's hunger for the supper. Piety and Charity, who had joint charge of the house from the Master of the house, held each a characteristic conversation with Christian, but it was left to Prudence to hold the most particular discourse with him until supper was ready, and it is to that so particular discourse that I much wish to turn your attention to-night.

With great tenderness, but at the same time with the greatest possible gravity, Prudence asked the pilgrim whether he did not still think sometimes of

[1] Delivered on the Sabbath before Communion.

the country from whence he had come out. Yes, he replied; how could I help thinking continually of that unhappy country and of my sad and miserable life in it; but, believe me,—or, rather, you cannot believe me,—with what shame and detestation I always think of my past life. My face burns as I now speak of my past life to you, and as I think what my old companions know and must often say about me. I detest, as you cannot possibly under-stand, every remembrance of my past life, and I hate and never can forgive myself, who, with mine own hands, so filled all my past life with shame and self-contempt. Gently stopping the remorseful pilgrim's self-accusations about his past life, Prudence asked him if he had not still with him, and, indeed, within him, some of the very things that had so destroyed both him and all his past life. ' Yes,' he honestly and humbly said. ' Yes, but greatly against my will : especially my inward and sinful cogita-tions.' At this Prudence looked on him with all her deep and soft eyes, for it was to this that she had been leading the conversation up all the time. Prudence had a great look of satisfaction, mingled with love and pity, at the way the pilgrim said ' especially my inward and sinful cogitations.' Those who stood by and observed Prudence wondered at her delight in the sad discourse on which the pilgrim now entered. But she had her own reasons for her delight in this particular kind of discourse, and it was seldom that she lighted on a pilgrim who both understood her questions and responded to them as did this man now sitting beside her. Now, my brethren, all parable apart, is that your religious experience? Are you full of shame and detestation at your inward cogitations? Are you tormented, enslaved, and downright cursed with your own evil thoughts? I do not ask whether or no you have such thoughts always within you. I do not ask, because I know. But I ask, because I would like to make sure that you know what, and the true nature of what, goes on incessantly in your mind and in your heart. Do you, or do you not, spit out your most inward thoughts ten times a day like poison? If you do, you are a truly religious man, and if you do not, you do not yet know the very ABC of true religion, and your dog has a better errand at the Lord's table than you have. And if your minister lets you sit down at the Lord's table without holding from time to time some particular discourse with you about your sinful thoughts, he is deceiving and misleading you, besides laying up for himself an awakening at last to shame and everlasting contempt. What a mill-stone his communion roll will be round such a minister's neck! And how his congregation will gnash their teeth at him when they see to what his miserable ministry has brought them!

Let a man examine himself, said Paul. What about your inward and sinful cogitations? asked Prudence. How long shall thy vain thoughts lodge within thee? demanded the bold prophet. Now, my brethren, what have you to say to that particular accusation? Do you know what vain thoughts are? Are you at all aware what multitudes of such thoughts lodge within you? Do they drive you every day to your knees, and do you blush with shame when you are alone before God at the fountain of folly that fills your mind and your heart continually? The Apostle speaks of vain hopes that make us ashamed that we ever entertained them. You have been often so ashamed, and yet do not such hopes still too easily arise in your heart? What castles of idiotic folly you still build! Were a sane man or a modest woman even to dream such dreams of folly overnight, they would blush and hide their heads all day at the thought. Out of a word, out of a look, out of what was neither a word nor a look intended for you, what a world of vanity will you build out of it! The question of Prudence is not whether or no you are still a born fool at heart, she does not put unnecessary questions: hers to you is the more pertinent and particular question, whether, since you left your former life and became a Christian, you feel every day increasing shame and detestation at yourself, on account of the vanity of your inward cogitations. My brethren, can you satisfy her who is set by her Master to hold particular discourse with all true Christians before supper? Can you say with the Psalmist,—could you tell Prudence where the Psalmist says,—I hate vain thoughts, but Thy law do I love? And can you silence her by telling her that her Master alone knows with what shame you think that He has such a fool as you are among His people?

Anger, also, sudden and even long-entertained anger, was one of the 'many failings' of which Christian was so conscious to himself. His outbursts of anger at home, he bitterly felt, might well be one of the causes why his wife and children did not accompany him on his pilgrimage. And though he knew his failing in this respect, and was very wary of it, yet he often failed even when he was most wary. Now, while anger is largely a result of our blood and temperament, yet few of us are so well-balanced and equable in our temperament and so pure and cool in our blood, as altogether to escape frequent outbursts of anger. The most happily constituted and the best governed of us have too much cause to be ashamed and penitent both before God and our neighbours for our outbursts of angry passion. But Prudence is so particular in her discourse before supper, that she goes far deeper into our anger than our wives and our children, our servants and our neighbours, can go. She not only asks if we stamp out the rising anger of our heart as we would stamp out sparks of fire in a house full of gunpowder ; but she insists on being told what we think of ourselves when the house of our heart is still so full of such fire and such gunpowder. Any man, to call a man, would be humbled in his own eyes and in his walk before his house at home after an explosion of anger among them ; but he who would satisfy Prudence and sit beside her at supper, must not only never let his anger kindle, but the simple secret heat of it, that fire of hell that is hid from all men but himself in the flint of his own hard and proud heart,—what, asks Prudence, do you think of that, and of yourself on account of that ? Does that keep you not only watchful and prayerful, but, what is the best ground in you of all true watchfulness and prayerfulness, full of secret shame, self-fear, and self-detestation ? One forenoon table would easily hold all our communicants if Prudence had the distribution of the tokens.

And, then, we who are true pilgrims, are of all men the most miserable, on account of that 'failing,' that rankling sting in our hearts, when any of our friends has more of this world's possessions, honours, and praises than we have, that pain at our neighbour's pleasure, that sickness at his health, that hunger for what we see him eat, that thirst for what we see him drink, that imprisonment of our spirits when we see him set at liberty, that depression at his exaltation, that sorrow at his joy, and joy at his sorrow, that evil heart that would have all things to itself. Yes, said Christian, I am only too conversant with all these sinful cogitations, but they are all greatly against my will, and might I but choose mine own thoughts, do you suppose that I would ever think these things any more? ' The cause is in my will,' said Cæsar, on a great occasion. But the true Christian, unhappily, cannot say that. If he could say that, he would soon say also that the snare is broken and that his soul has escaped. And then the cause of all his evil cogitations, his vain thoughts, his angry feelings, his envious feelings, his ineradicable covetousness, his hell-rooted and heaven-towering pride, and his whole evil heart of unbelief would soon be at an end. 'I cannot be free of sin,' said Thomas Boston, 'but God knows that He would be welcome to make havoc of my lusts to-night and to make me henceforth a holy man. I know no lust that I would not be content to part with. My will bound hand and foot I desire to lay at His feet.' Yes: such is the mystery and depth of sin in the

hearts of all God's saints, that far deeper than their
will, far back behind their will, the whole substance
and very core of their hearts is wholly corrupt and
enslaved to sin. And thus it is that while their
renewed and delivered will works out, so far, their
salvation in their walk and conversation among men,
the helplessness of their will in the cleansing and
the keeping of their hearts is to the end the sorrow
and the mystery of their sanctification. To will was
present with Paul, and with Bunyan, and with
Boston; but their heart—they could not with all
their keeping keep their heart. No man can; no
man who has at all tried it can. 'Might I but
choose mine own thoughts, I would choose never
to think of these things more: but when I would
be doing of that which is best, that which is worst
is with me.' We can choose almost all things.
Our will and choice have almost all things at their
disposal. We can choose our God. We can choose
life or death. We can choose heaven or hell. We
can choose our church, our minister, our books, our
companions, our words, our works, and, to some
extent, our inward thoughts, but only to some
extent. We can encourage this or that thought;
we can entertain it and dwell upon it; or we can
detect it, detest it, and cast it out. But that secret
place in our heart where our thoughts hide and
harbour, and out of which they spring so suddenly
upon the mind and the heart, the imagination
and the conscience,—of that secretest of all secret
places, God alone is able to say, I search the heart.
'As for secret thoughts,' says our author, speaking of
his own former religious life, 'I took no notice of

them, neither did I understand what Satan's temptations were, nor how they were to be withstood and resisted.' But now all these things are his deepest grief, as they are ours,—as many of us as have been truly turned in our deepest hearts to God.

'But,' replied Prudence, 'do you not find sometimes as if those things were vanquished which at other times are your perplexity?' 'Yes, but that is but seldom; but they are to me golden hours in which such things happen to me.' 'Can you remember by what means you find your annoyances at times as if they were vanquished?' 'Yes, when I think what I saw at the cross, that will do it; and when I look upon my broidered coat, that will do it; also, when I look into the roll that I carry in my bosom, that will do it; and when my thoughts wax warm about whither I am going, that will do it.' Yes; and these same things have many a time done it to ourselves also. We also, my brethren—let me tell you your own undeniable experience—we also have such golden hours sometimes, when we feel as if we should never again have such an evil heart within us. The Cross of Christ to us also has done it. It is of such golden hours that Isaac Watts sings in his noble hymn:

'When I survey the wondrous Cross;'

and as often as we sing that hymn with our eyes upon the object, that will for a time vanquish our worst cogitations. Also, when we read the roll that we too carry in our bosom—that is to say, when we go back into our past life till we see it and feel it all, and till we can think and speak of nothing else but the sin that abounded in it and the grace that much more abounded, that has a thousand times given us also golden hours, even rest from our own evil hearts. And we also have often made our hearts too hot for sin to show itself, when we read our hearts deep into such books as *The Paradiso, The Pilgrim's Progress, The Saints' Rest, The Serious Call, The Religious Affections,* and such like. These books have often vanquished our annoyances, and given us golden hours on the earth. Yes, but that is but seldom.

'Now, what is it,' asked Prudence, as she wound up this so particular colloquy, 'that makes you so desirous to go to Mount Zion?'

'Why,' replied the pilgrim, and the water stood in his eyes, 'why, there I hope to see Him alive that did hang dead on the cross; and there I hope to be rid of all those things that to this day are an annoyance to me; there they say is no death, and there shall I dwell with such company as I love best. For, to tell you truth, I love Him, because by Him I was eased of my burden, and I am weary of my inward sickness; and I would fain be where I shall die no more, and for ever with that company that shall continually cry, Holy, holy, holy.'

XVI

CHARITY

' I will walk within my house with a perfect heart.'—David.

HERE can be nobody here to-night so stark stupid as to suppose that the pilgrim had run away from home and left his wife and children to the work-house. There have been wiseacres who have found severe fault with John Bunyan because he made his Puritan pilgrim such a bad husband and such an unnatural father. But nobody possessed of a spark of common sense, not to say religion or literature, would ever commit himself to such an utter imbecility as that. John Bunyan's pilgrim, whatever he may have been before he became a pilgrim, all the time he was a pilgrim, was the most faithful, affectionate, and solicitous husband in all the country round about, and the tenderest, the most watchful, and the wisest of fathers. This pilgrim stayed all the more at home that he went so far away from home; he accomplished his whole wonderful pilgrimage beside his own forge and at his own fireside; and he entered the Celestial City amid trumpets and bells and harps and psalms, while all the time sleeping in his own humble bed. The House Beautiful, there-fore, to which we have now come in his company, is not some remote and romantic mansion away up among the mountains a great many days' journey distant from this poor man's everyday home. The House Beautiful was nothing else,—what else better, what else so good could it be?—than just this Christian man's first communion Sabbath and his first communion table (first, that is, after his true conversion from sin to God and his confessed entrance into a new life), while the country from whence he had come out, and concerning which both Piety and Prudence catechised him so closely, was just his former life of open ungodliness and all his evil walk and conversation while he was as yet living without God and without hope in the world. The country on which he confessed that he now looked back with so much shame and detestation was not England or Bedfordshire, but the wicked life he had lived in that land and in that shire. And when Charity asked him as to whether he was a married man and had a family, she knew quite well that he was, only she made a pretence of asking him those domestic questions in order thereby to start the touching conversation.

Beginning, then, at home, as she always began, Charity said to Christian, 'Have you a family? Are you a married man?' 'I have a wife and four small children,' answered Christian. 'And why did you not bring them with you?' Then Christian wept and said, 'Oh, how willingly would I have done so, but they were all of them utterly averse to my going on pilgrimage.' 'But you should have talked to them and have shown them their danger.' 'So I did,' he replied, 'but I seemed to them as one that mocked.' Now, this of talking, and, especially, of talking about religious things to children, is one of the most difficult things in the world,—that is, to do it well. Some people have the happy knack of talking to their own and to other people's children so as always to interest and impress them. But such happy people are few. Most people talk at their children whenever they begin to talk to them, and thus, without knowing it, they nauseate their children with their conversation altogether. To respect a little child, to stand in some awe of a little child, to choose your topics, your opportunities, your neighbourhood, your moods and his as well as all your words, and always to speak your sincerest, simplest, most straightforward and absolutely wisest is indispensable with a child. Take your mannerisms, your condescensions, your affectations, your moralisings, and all your insincerities to your debauched equals, but bring your truest and your best to your child. Unless you do so, you will be sure to lay yourself open to a look that will suddenly go through you, and that will swiftly convey to you that your child sees through you and despises you and your conversation too. 'You should not only have talked to your children of their danger,' said Charity, 'but you should have shown them their danger.' Yes, Charity; but a man must himself see his own and his children's danger too, before he can show it to them, as well as see it clearly at the time he is trying to show it to them. And how many fathers, do you suppose, have the eyes to see such danger, and how then can they shew such danger to their children, of all people? Once get fathers to see dangers or anything else aright, and then you will not need to tell them how they are to instruct and impress their children. Nature herself will then tell them how to talk to their children, and when Nature teaches, all our children will immediately and unweariedly listen.

But, especially, said Charity, as your boys grew up—I think you said that you had four boys and no girls?—well, then, all the more, as they grew up, you should have taken occasion to talk to them about yourself. Did your little boy never petition you for a story about yourself; and as he grew up did you never confide to him what you have never confided to his mother? Something, as I was saying, that made you sad when you were a boy and a rising man, with a sadness your son can still see in you as you talk to him. In conversations like that a boy finds out what a friend he has in his father, and his father from that day has his best friend in his son. And then as Matthew grew up and began to out-grow his brothers and to form friendships out of doors, did you study to talk at the proper time to him, and on subjects on which you never venture to talk about to any other boy or man? You men, Charity went on to say, live in a world of your own, and though we women are well out of it, yet we cannot be wholly ignorant that it is there. And, we may well be wrong, but we cannot but think that fathers, if not mothers, might safely tell their men-children at least more than they do tell them of the sure dangers that lie straight in their way, of the sorrow that men and women bring on one another, and of what is the destruction of so many cities. We may well be wrong, for we are only women, but I have told you what we all think who keep this house and hear the reports and repentances of pilgrims, both Piety and Prudence and I myself. And I, for one, largely agree with the three women. It is easier said than done. But the simple saying of it may perhaps lead some fathers and mothers to think about it, and to ask whether or no it is desirable and advisable to do it, which of them is to attempt it, on what occasion, and to what extent. Christian by this time had the Slough of Despond with all its history and all that it contained to tell his eldest son about; he had the wicket gate also just above the slough, the hill Difficulty, the Interpreter's House, the place somewhat ascending with a cross standing upon it, and a little below, in the bottom, a sepulchre, not to speak of her who assaulted Faithful, whose name was Wanton, and who at one time was like to have done even that trusty pilgrim a life-long mischief. Christian rather boasted to Charity of his wariness, especially in the matter of his children's amusements, but Charity seemed to think that he had carried his wariness into other matters besides amusements, without the best possible results there either. I have sometimes thought with her that among our multitude of congresses and conferences of all kinds of people and upon all manner of subjects, room and membership might have been found for a conference of fathers and mothers. Fathers to give and take counsel about how to talk to their sons, and mothers to their daughters. I am much of Charity's mind, that, if more were done at home, and done with some frankness, for our sons and daughters, there would be fewer fathers and mothers found sitting at the Lord's table alone. 'You should have talked to them,' said Charity, with some severity in her tones, 'and, especially, you should have told them of your own sorrow.'

And then, coming still closer up to Christian, Charity asked him whether he prayed, both before and after he so spoke to his children, that God would bless what he said to them. Charity believeth all things, hopeth all things, but when she saw this man about to sit down all alone at the supper table, it took Charity all her might to believe that he had both spoken to his children and at the same time prayed to God for them as he ought to have done. Our old ministers used to lay this vow on all fathers and mothers at the time of baptism, that they were to pray both with and for their children. Now, that is a fine formula; it is a most comprehensive, and, indeed, exhaustive formula. Both with and for. And especially with. With, at such and such times, on such and such occasions, and in such and such places. At those times, say, when your boy has told a lie, or struck his little brother, or stolen something, or destroyed something. To pray with him at such times, and to pray with him properly, and, if you feel able to do it, and are led to do it, to tell him something after the prayer about yourself, and your own not-yet-forgotten boyhood, and your father; it makes a fine time to mix talk and prayer together in that way. Charity is not easily provoked, but the longer she lives and keeps the table in the House Beautiful the more she is provoked to think that there is far too little prayer among pilgrims; far too little of all kinds of prayer, but especially prayer with and for their children. But hard as it was to tell all the truth at that moment about Christian's past walk in his house at home, yet he was able with the simple truth to say that he had indeed prayed both with and for his children, and that, as they knew and could not but remember, not seldom. Yes, he said, I did sometimes so pray with my boys, and that too, as you may believe, with much affection, for you must think that my four boys were all very dear to me. And it is my firm belief that all that good man's boys will come right yet: Matthew and Joseph and James and Samuel and all. 'With much affection.' I like that. I have unbounded faith in those prayers, both for and with, in which there is much affection. It is want of affection, and want of imagination, that shipwrecks so many of our prayers. But this man's prayers had both these elements of sure success in them, and they must come at last to harbour. At that one word 'with much affection,' this man's closet door flies open and I see the old pilgrim first alone, and then with his arms round his eldest son's neck, and both father and son weeping together till they are ashamed to appear at supper till they have washed their faces and got their most smiling and everyday looks put on again. You just wait and see if Matthew and all the four boys down to the last do not escape into the Celestial City before the gate is shut. And when it is asked, Who are these and whence came they? listen to their song and you will hear those four happy children saying that their father, when they were yet boys, both talked with them and prayed for and with them with so much affection that therefore they are before the throne.

Why, then, with such a father and with such makable boys, why was this household brought so near everlasting shipwreck? It was the mother that did it. In one word, it was the wife and the mother that did it. It was the mistress of the house who wrought the mischief here. She was a poor woman, she was a poor man's wife, and one would have thought that she had little enough temptation to hang upon this present world. But there it was, she did hang upon it as much as if she had been the mother of the finest daughters and the most promising boys in all the town. Things like this were from time to time reported to her by her neighbours. One fine lady had been heard to say that she would never have for her tradesman any man who frequented conventicles, who was not content with the religion of his betters, and who must needs scorn the parish church and do despite to the saints' days. Another gossip asked her what she expected to make of her great family of boys when it was well known that all the gentry in the neighbourhood but two or three had sworn that they would never have a hulking Puritan to brush their boots or run their errands. And it almost made her husband burn his book and swear that he would never be seen at another prayer-meeting when his wife so often said to him that he should never have had children, that he should never have made her his wife, and that he was not like this when they were first man and wife. And in her bitterness she would name this wife or that maid, and would say, You should have married her. She would have gone to the meeting-house with you as often as you wished. Her sons are far enough from good service to please you. ‘My wife,’ he softly said, ‘was afraid of losing the world. And then, after that, my growing sons were soon given over, all I could do, to the foolish delights of youth, so that, what by one thing and what by another, they left me to wander in this manner alone.’ And I suppose there is scarcely a household among ourselves where there have not been serious and damaging misunderstandings between old-fashioned fathers and their young people about what the old people called the ‘foolish delights’ of their sons and daughters. And in thinking this matter over, I have often been struck with how Job did when his sons and his daughters were bent upon feasting and dancing in their eldest brother's house. The old man did not lay an interdict upon the entertainment. He did not take part in it, but neither did he absolutely forbid it. If it must be it must be, said the wise patriarch. And since I do not know whom they may meet there, or what they may be tempted to do, I will sanctify them all. I will not go up into my bed till I have prayed for all my seven sons and three daughters, each one of them by their names; and till they come home safely I will rise every morning and offer burnt-offerings according to the number of them all. And do you think that those burnt-offerings and accompanying intercessions would go for nothing

when the great wind came from the wilderness
and smote the four corners of the banqueting-
house? If you cannot banish the love of foolish
delights out the hearts of your sons and daughters,
then do not quarrel with them over such things; a
family quarrel in a Christian man's house is surely
far worse than a feast or a dance. Only, if they
must feast and dance and such like, be you all the
more diligent in your exercises at home on their
behalf till they are back again, where, after all,
they like best to be, in their good, kind, liberal,
and loving father's house.

Have you a family? Are you a married man? Or,
if not, do you hope one day to be? Then attend
betimes to what Charity says to Christian in the
House Beautiful, and not less to what he says
back again to her.

XVII

SHAME

'Whosoever shall be ashamed of Me, and of My words, of him shall the Son of Man be ashamed, when He shall come in His own glory, and in His Father's, and of the holy angels.'—*Our Lord.*

SHAME has not got the attention that it deserves either from our moral philosophers or from our practical and experimental divines. And yet it would well repay both classes of students to attend far more to shame. For, what really is shame? Shame is an original instinct planted in our souls by our Maker, and intended by Him to act as a powerful and pungent check to our doing of any act that is mean or dishonourable in the eyes of our fellow-men. Shame is a kind of social conscience. Shame is a secondary sense of sin. In shame, our imagination becomes a kind of moral sense. Shame sets up in our bosom a not undivine tribunal, which judges us and sentences us in the absence or the silence of nobler and more awful sanctions and sentences. But then, as things now are with us, like all the rest of the machinery of the soul, shame has gone sadly astray both in its objects and in its operations, till it demands a long, a severe, and a very noble discipline over himself before any man can keep shame in its proper place and directed in upon its proper objects. In the present disorder of our souls, we are all acutely ashamed of many things that are not the proper objects of shame at all; while, on the other hand, we feel no shame at all at multitudes of things that are really most blameworthy, dishonourable, and contemptible. We are ashamed of things in our lot and in our circumstances that, if we only knew it, are our opportunity and our honour; we are ashamed of things that are the clear will and the immediate dispensation of Almighty God. And, then, we feel no shame at all at the most dishonourable things, and that simply because the men around us are too coarse in their morals and too dull in their sensibilities to see any shame in such things. And thus it comes about that, in the very best of men, their still perverted sense of shame remains in them a constant snare and a source of temptation. A man of a fine nature feels keenly the temptation to shrink from those paths of truth and duty that expose him to the cruel judgments and the coarse and scandalising attacks of public and private enemies. It was in the Valley of Humiliation that Shame set upon Faithful, and it is a real humiliation to any man of anything of this pilgrim's fine character and feeling to be attacked, scoffed at, and held up to blame and opprobrium. And the finer and the more affectionate any man's heart and character are, the more he feels and shrinks from the coarse treatment this world gives to those whom it has its own reasons to hate and assail. They had the stocks and the pillory and the shears

in Bunyan's rude and uncivilised day, by means
of which many of the best men of that day were
exposed to the insults and brutalities of the mob.
The newspapers would be the pillory of our day,
were it not that, on the whole, the newspaper press
is conducted with such scrupulous fairness and with
a love of truth and justice such that no man need
shrink from the path of duty through fear of insult
and injury.

But it is time to come to the encounter between
Shame and Faithful in the Valley of Humiliation.
Shame, properly speaking, is not one of our Bunyan
gallery of portraits at all. Shame, at best, is but a
kind of secondary character in this dramatic book.
We do not meet with Shame directly; we only
hear about him through the report of Faithful.
That first-class pilgrim was almost overcome of
Shame, so hot was their encounter; and it is the
extraordinarily feeling, graphic, and realistic account
of their encounter that Faithful gives us that has
led me to take up Shame for our reproof and correction to-night.

Religion altogether, but especially all personal
religion, said Shame to Faithful, is an unmanly
business. There is a certain touch of smallness
and pitifulness, he said, in all religion, but especially in experimental religion. It brings a man into
junctures and into companionships, and it puts
offices and endurances upon one such as try a
man if he has any greatness of spirit about him
at all. This life on which you are entering, said
Shame, will cost you many a blush before you are
done with it. You will lay yourself open to many a

scoff. The Puritan religion, and all the ways of that religious fraternity, are peculiarly open to the shafts of ridicule. Now, all that was quite true. There was no denying the truth of what Shame said. And Faithful felt the truth of it all, and felt it most keenly, as he confessed to Christian. The blood came into my face as the fellow spake, and what he said for a time almost beat me out of the upward way altogether. But in this dilemma also all true Christians can fall back, as Faithful fell back, upon the example of their Master. In this as in every other experience of temptation and endurance, our Lord is the forerunner and the example of His people. Our Lord was in all points tempted like as we are, and among all His other temptations He was tempted to be ashamed of His work on earth and of the life and the death His work led Him into. He must have often felt ashamed at the treatment He received during His life of humiliation, as it is well called ; and He must often have felt ashamed of His disciples : but all that is blotted out by the crowning shame of the cross. We hang our worst criminals rather than behead or shoot them, in order to heap up the utmost possible shame and disgrace upon them, as well as to execute justice upon them. And what the hangman's rope is in our day, all that the cross was in our Lord's day. And, then, as if the cross itself was not shame enough, all the circumstances connected with His cross were planned and carried out so as to heap the utmost possible shame and humiliation upon His head. Our prison warders have to watch the murderers in their cells night and day, lest they should take their own life in order to escape the hangman's rope; but our Lord, keenly as He felt His coming shame, said to His horrified disciples, Behold, we go up to Jerusalem, when the Son of Man shall be mocked, and spitefully entreated, and spitted on; and they shall scourge Him and put Him to death. Do you ever think of your Lord in His shame? How they made a fool of Him, as we say. How they took off His own clothes and put on Him now a red cloak and now a white; how they put a sword of lath in His hand, and a crown of thorns on His head; how they bowed the knee before Him, and asked royal favours from Him; and then how they spat in His face, and struck Him on the cheek, while the whole house rang with shouts of laughter. And, then, the last indignity of man, how they stripped Him naked and lashed His naked and bleeding body to a whipping-post. And how they wagged their heads and put out their tongues at Him when He was on the tree, and invited Him to come down and preach to them now, and they would all become His disciples. Did not Shame say the simple truth when he warned Faithful that religion had always and from the beginning made its followers the ridicule of their times?

If you are really going to be a religious man, Shame went on, you will have to carry about with you a very tender conscience, and a more unmanly and miserable thing than a tender conscience I cannot conceive. A tender conscience will cost you something, let me tell you, to keep it. If nothing else, a tender conscience will all your life long expose you to the mockery and the contempt of all the brave spirits of the time. That also is true. At any rate, a tender conscience will undoubtedly compel its possessor to face the brave spirits of the time. There is a good story told to this present point about Sir Robert Peel, a Prime Minister of our Queen. When a young man, Peel was one of the guests at a select dinner-party in the West-end of London. And after the ladies had left the table the conversation of the gentlemen took a turn such that it could not have taken as long as the ladies were present. Peel took no share in the stories or the merriment that went on, and, at last, he rose up and ordered his carriage, and, with a burning face, left the room. When he was challenged as to why he had broken up the pleasant party so soon, he could only reply that his conscience would not let him stay any longer. No doubt Peel felt the mocking laughter that he left behind him, but, as Shame said to Faithful, the tenderness of the young statesman's conscience compelled him to do as he did. But we are not all Peels. And there are plenty of workshops and offices and dinner-tables in our own city, where young men who would walk up to the cannon's mouth without flinching have not had Peel's courage to protest against indecency or to confess that they belonged to an evangelical church. If a church is only sufficiently unevangelical there is no trial of conscience or of courage in confessing that you belong to it. But as Shame so ably and honestly said, that type of religion that creates a tender conscience in its followers, and sets them to watch their words and their ways, and makes them tie themselves up from all hectoring liberty—to choose that religion, and to cleave to it to the end, will make a young man the ridicule still of all the brave spirits round about him. Ambitious young men get promotion and reward every day among us for desertions and apostasies in religion, for which, if they had been guilty of the like in war, they would have been shot. 'And so you are a Free Churchman, I am told.' That was all that was said. But the sharp youth understood without any more words, and he made his choice accordingly; till it is becoming a positive surprise to find the rising members of certain professions in certain churches. The Quakers have a proverb in England that a family carriage never drives for two generations past the parish church door. Of which state of matters Shame showed himself a shrewd prophet two hundred years ago when he said that but few of the rich and the mighty and the wise remained long of Faithful's Puritan opinion unless they were first persuaded to be fools, and to be of a voluntary fondness to venture the loss of all.

And I will tell you two other things, said sharp-sighted and plain-spoken Shame, that your present religion will compel you to do if you adhere to it. It will compel you from time to time to ask your neighbour's forgiveness even for petty faults, and it will insist with you that you make restitution when you have done the weak and the friendless any hurt or any wrong. And every manly mind will tell you that life is not worth having on such humbling terms as those are. Whatever may be thought about Shame in other respects, it cannot be denied that he had a sharp eye for the facts of life, and a shrewd tongue in setting those facts forth. He has hit the blot exactly in the matter of our first duty to our neighbour; he has put his finger on one of the matters where so many of us, through a false shame, come short. It costs us a tremendous struggle with our pride to go to our neighbour and to ask his forgiveness for a fault, petty fault or other. Did you ever do it? When did you do it last, to whom, and for what? One Sabbath morning, now many years ago, I had occasion to urge this elementary evangelical duty on my people here, and I did it as plainly as I could. Next day one of my young men, who is now a devoted and honoured elder, came to me and told me that he had done that morning what his conscience yesterday told him in the church to do. He had gone to a neighbour's place of business, had asked for an interview, and had begged his neighbour's pardon. I am sure neither of those two men have forgotten that moment, and the thought of it has often since nerved me to speak plainly about some of their most unwelcome duties to my people. Shame, no doubt, pulled back my noble friend's hand when it was on the office bell, but, like Faithful in the text, he shook him out of his company and went in. I spoke of the remarkable justice of the newspaper press in the opening of these remarks. And it so happens that, as I lay down my pen to rest my hand after writing this sentence and lift a London evening paper, I read this editorial note, set within the well-known brackets at the end of an indignant and expostulatory letter: ['Our correspondent's complaint is just. The paragraph imputing bad motives should not have been admitted.'] I have no doubt that editor felt some shame as he handed that apologetic note to the printer. But not to speak of any other recognition and recompense, he has the recompense of the recognition of all honourable-minded men who have read that honourable admission and apology.

Shame was quite right in his scoff about restitution also. For restitution rings like a trumpet tone through the whole of the law of Moses, and then the New Testament republishes that law if only in the exquisite story of Zaccheus. And, indeed, take it altogether, I do not know where to find in the same space a finer vindication of Puritan pulpit ethics than just in this taunting and terrifying attack on Faithful. There is no better test of true religion both as it is preached and practised than just to ask for and to grant forgiveness, and to offer and accept restitution. Now, does your public and private life defend and adorn your minister's pulpit in these two so practical matters? Could your minister point to you as a proof of the ethics of evangelical teaching? Can any one in this city speak up in defence of your church and thus protest: 'Say what you like about that church and its ministers, all I can say is, that its members know how to make an apology; as, also, how to pay back with interest what they at one time damaged or defrauded'? Can any old creditor's widow or orphan stand up for our doctrine and defend our discipline pointing to you? If you go on to be a Puritan, said Shame to Faithful, you will have to ask your neighbour's forgive-

ness even for petty faults, and you will have to
make restitution with usury where you have taken
anything from any one, and how will you like that?

And what did you say to all this, my brother?
Say? I could not tell what to say at the first. I
felt my blood coming up into my face at some of
the things that Shame said and threatened. But,
at last, I began to consider that that which is highly
esteemed among men is often had in abomination
with God. And I said to myself again, Shame tells
me what men do and what men think, but he has
told me nothing about what He thinks with Whom
I shall soon have alone to do. Therefore, thought
I, what God thinks and says is wisest and best, let
all the men of the world say what they will. Let
all false shame, then, depart from my heart, for how
else shall I look upon my Lord, and how shall He
look upon me at His coming?

XVIII

TALKATIVE

'A man full of talk.'—*Zophar.*
'Let thy words be few.'—*The Preacher.*
'The soul of religion is the practick part.'—*Christian.*

INCE we all have a tongue, and since so much of our time is taken up with talk, a simple catalogue of the sins of the tongue is enough to terrify us. The sins of the tongue take up a much larger space in the Bible than we would believe till we have begun to suffer from other men's tongues and especially from our own. The Bible speaks a great deal more and a great deal plainer about the sins of the tongue than any of our pulpits dare to do. In the Psalms alone you would think that the psalmists scarcely suffer from anything else worth speaking about but the evil tongues of their friends and of their enemies. The Book of Proverbs also is full of the same lashing scourge. And James the Just, in a passage of terrible truth and power, tells us that we are already as good as perfect men if we can bridle our tongue; and that, on the other hand, if we do not bridle our tongue, all our seeming to be religious is a sham and a self-deception,—that man's religion is vain.

With many men and many women great talkativeness is a matter of simple temperament and mental constitution. And a talkative habit would be a childlike and an innocent habit if the heart of the talker and the hearts of those to whom he talks so much were only full of truth and love. But our hearts and our neighbours' hearts being what they are, in the multitude of words there wanteth not sin. So much of our talk is about our absent neighbours, and there are so many misunderstandings, prejudices, ambitions, competitions, oppositions, and all kinds of cross-interests between us and our absent neighbours, that we cannot long talk about them till our hearts have run our tongues into all manner of trespass. Bishop Butler discourses on the great dangers that beset a talkative temperament with almost more than all his usual sagacity, seriousness, and depth. And those who care to see how the greatest of our modern moralists deals with their besetting sin should lose no time in possessing and mastering Butler's great discourse. It is a truly golden discourse, and it ought to be read at least once a month by all the men and all the women who have tongues in their heads. Bishop Butler points out to his offending readers, in a way they can never forget, the certain mischief they do to themselves and to other people just by talking too much. But there are far worse sins that our tongues fall into than the bad enough sins that spring out of impertinent and unrestrained loquacity. There are many times when our talk, long or short, is already simple and downright evil. It is ten to one, it is a hundred to one, that you do not know and would not believe how much you fall every day and in every conversation into one or other of the sins of the tongue. If you would only begin to see and accept this, that every time you speak or hear about your absent neighbour what you would not like him to speak or hear about you, you are in that a talebearer, a slanderer, a backbiter, or a liar,—when you begin to see and admit that about yourself, you will not wonder at what the Bible says with such bitter indignation about the diabolical sins of the tongue. If you would just begin to-night to watch yourselves—on the way home from church, at home after the day is over, to-morrow morning when the letters and the papers are opened, and so on,—how instinctively, incessantly, irrepressibly you speak about the absent in a way you would be astounded and horrified to be told they were at that moment speaking about you, then you would soon be wiser than all your teachers in the sins and in the government of the tongue. And you would seven times every day pluck out your tongue before God till He gives it back to you clean and kind in that land where all men shall love their neighbours, present and absent, as themselves.

Take detraction for an example, one of the commonest, and, surely, one of the most detestable of the sins of the tongue. And the etymology here, as in this whole region, is most instructive and most impressive. In detraction you *draw away* something from your neighbour that is most precious and most dear to him. In detraction you are a thief, and a thief of the falsest and wickedest kind. For your neighbour's purse is trash, while his good name is far more precious to him than all his gold. Some one praises your neighbour in your hearing, his talents, his performances, his character, his motives, or something else that belongs to your neighbour. Some one does that in your hearing who either does not know you, or who wishes to torture and expose you, and you fall straight into the snare thus set for you, and begin at once to belittle, depreciate, detract from, and run down your neighbour, who has been too much praised for your peace of mind and your self-control. You insinuate something to his disadvantage and dishonour. You quote some authority you have heard to his hurt. And so on past all our power to picture you. For detraction has a thousand devices taught to it by the master of all such devices, wherewith to drag down and defile the great and the good. But with all you can say or do, you cannot for many days get out of your mind the heart-poisoning praise you heard spoken of your envied neighbour. Never praise any potter's pots in the hearing of another potter, said the author of the *Nicomachean Ethics.* Aristotle said potter's pots, but he really all the time was thinking of a philosopher's books; only he said potter's pots to draw off his readers' attention from himself. Now, always remember that ancient and wise advice. Take care how you praise a potter's pots, a philosopher's books, a woman's beauty, a speaker's speech, a preacher's sermon to another potter, philosopher, woman, speaker, or preacher; unless, indeed, you maliciously wish secretly to torture them, or publicly to expose them, or, if their sanctification is begun, to sanctify them to their most inward and spiritual sanctification.

Backbiting, again, would seem at first sight to be a sin of the teeth rather than of the tongue, only, no sharpest tooth can tear you when your back is turned like your neighbour's evil tongue. Pascal has many dreadful things about the corruption and misery of man, but he has nothing that strikes its terrible barb deeper into all our consciences than this, that if all our friends only knew what we have said about them behind their back, we would not have four friends in all the world. Neither we would. I know I would not have one. How many would you have? And who would they be? You cannot name them. I defy you to name them. They do not exist. The tongue can no man tame.

'Giving of characters' also takes up a large part of our everyday conversation. We cannot well help characterising, describing, and estimating one another. But, as far as possible, when we see the conversation again approaching that dangerous subject, we should call to mind our past remorse; we should suppose our absent neighbour present; we should imagine him in our place and ourselves in his place, and so turn the rising talk into another channel. For, the truth is, few of us are able to do justice to our neighbour when we begin to discuss and describe him. Generosity in our talk is far easier for us than justice. It was this incessant giving of characters that our Lord had in His eye when He said in His Sermon on the Mount, Judge not. But our Lord might as well never have uttered that warning word for all the attention we give it. For we go on judging one another and sentencing one another as if we were entirely and in all things blameless ourselves, and as if God had set us up in our blamelessness in His seat of judgment over all our fellows. How seldom do we hear any one say in a public debate or in a private conversation, I don't know; or, It is no matter of mine; or, I feel that I am not in possession of all the facts; or, It may be so, but I must not judge. We never hear such things as these said. No one pays the least attention to the Preacher on the Mount. And if any one says to us, I must not judge, we never forgive him, because his humility and his obedience so condemn all our ill-formed, prejudiced, rash, and ill-natured judgments of our neighbour. Since, therefore, so Butler sums up, it is so hard for us to enter on our neighbour's character without offending the law of Christ, we should learn to decline that kind of conversation altogether, and determine to get over that strong inclination most of us have, to be continually talking about the concerns, the behaviour, and the deserts of our neighbours.

Now, it was all those vices of the tongue in full outbreak in the day of James the Just that made that apostle, half in sorrow, half in anger, demand of all his readers that they should henceforth begin to bridle their tongues. And, like all that most practical apostle's counsels, that is a most impressive and memorable commandment. For, it is well known that all sane men who either ride on or drive unruly horses, take good care to bridle their horses well before they bring them out of their stable door. And then they keep their bridle-hand firm closed on the bridle-rein till their horses are back in the stable again. Especially and particularly they keep a close eye and a firm hand on their horse's bridle on all steep inclines and at all sharp angles and sudden turns in the road; when sudden trains are passing and when stray dogs are barking. If the rider or the driver of a horse did not look at nothing else but the bridle of his horse, both he and his horse under him would soon be in the ditch,—as so many of us are at the present moment because we have an untamed tongue in our mouth on which we have not yet begun to put the bridle of truth and justice and brotherly love. Indeed, such woe and misery has an untamed tongue wrought in other churches and in other and more serious ages than ours, that special religious brotherhoods have been banded together just on the special and strict engagement that they would above all things put a bridle on their tongues. 'What are the chief cares of a young convert?' asked such a convert at an aged Carthusian. 'I said I will take heed to my ways that I trespass not with my tongue,' replied the saintly father. 'Say no more for the present,' interrupted the youthful beginner; 'I will go home and practise that, and will come again when I have performed it.'

Now, whatever faults that tall man had who took up so much of Faithful's time and attention, he was a saint compared with the men and the women who have just passed before us. Talkative, as John

Bunyan so scornfully names that tall man, though he undoubtedly takes up too much time and too much space in Bunyan's book, was not a busybody in other men's matters at any rate. Nobody could call him a detractor or a backbiter or a talebearer or a liar. Christian knew him well, and had known him long, but Christian was not afraid to leave him alone with Faithful. We all know men we feel it unsafe to leave long alone with our friends. We feel sure that they will be talking about us, and that to our hurt, as soon as our backs are about. But to give that tall man his due, he was not given with all his talk to talebearing or scandal or detraction. Had he been guilty of any of these things, Faithful would soon have found him out, and would have left him to go to the Celestial City by himself. But, after talking for half a day with Talkative, instead of finding out anything wrong in the tall man's talk, Faithful was so taken and so struck with it, that he stepped across to Christian and said, 'What a brave companion we have got! Surely this man will make a most excellent pilgrim!' 'So I once thought too,' said Christian, 'till I went to live beside him, and have to do with him in the business of daily life.' Yes, it is near neighbourhood and the business of everyday life that try a talking man. If you go to a meeting for prayer, and hear some men praying and speaking on religious subjects, you would say to yourself, What a good man that is, and how happy must his wife and children and servants and neighbours be with such an example always before them, and with such an intercessor for them always with God! But if you were to go home with that so devotional man, and try to do business with him, and were compelled to cross him and go against him, you would find out why Christian smiled so when Faithful was so full of Talkative's praises.

But of all the religiously-loquacious men of our day, your ministers are the chief. For your ministers must talk in public, and that often and at great length, whether they are truly religious men at home or no. It is their calling to talk to you unceasingly about religious matters. You chose them to be your ministers because they could talk well. You would not put up with a minister who could not talk well on religious things. You estimate them by their talk. You praise and pay them by their talk. And if they are to live, talk incessantly to you about religion they must, and they do. If any other man among us is not a religious man, well, then, he can at least hold his tongue. There is no necessity laid on him to speak in public about things that he does not practise at home. But we hard-bested ministers must go on speaking continually about the most solemn things. And if we are not extraordinarily watchful over ourselves, and extraordinarily and increasingly conscientious, if we are not steadily growing in inwardness and insight and depth and real spirituality of mind and life ourselves, we cannot escape,—our calling in life will not let us escape,—becoming as sounding brass. There is an awful sentence in Butler that should be written in letters of fire in every minister's conscience, to the effect that continually going over religion in talk and making fine pictures of it in the pulpit, creates a professional insensibility to personal religion that is the everlasting ruin of multitudes of eloquent ministers. That is true. We ministers all feel that to be true. Our miserable experience tells us that is only too true of ourselves. What a flood of demoralising talk has been poured out from the pulpits of this one city to-day!—demoralising to preachers and to hearers both, because not intended to be put in practice. How few of those who have talked and heard talk all this day about divine truth and human duty, have made the least beginning or the least resolve to live as they have spoken and heard! And, yet, all will in words again admit that the soul of religion is the practick part, and that the tongue without the heart and the life is but death and corruption.

Let us, then, this very night begin to do something practical after all this talk about talk. And let us all begin to do something in the direct line of our present talk. What a noble congregation of evangelical Carthusians that would make us if we all put a bridle on our tongue to-night before we left this house. For we all have neighbours, friends, enemies, against whom we every day sin with our unbridled tongue. We all have acquaintances we are ashamed to meet, we have been so unkind and so unjust to them with our tongue. We hang down our head when they shake our hand. Yes, we know the men quite well of whom Pascal speaks. We know many men who would never speak to us again if they only knew how, and how often, we have spoken about them behind their back. Well, let us sin against them, and against ourselves, and against our Master's command and example no more. Let this night and this lecture on Talkative and his kindred see the last of our sin against our ill-used neighbour. Let us promise God and our own consciences tonight, that we shall all this week put on a bridle about that man, and about that subject, and in that place, and in that company. Let us say, God helping me, I shall for all this week not speak about that man at all, anything either good or bad, nor on that subject, nor will I let the conversation turn into that channel at all if I can help it. And God will surely help us, till, after weeks and years of such prayer and such practice, we shall by slow degrees, and after many defeats, be able to say with the Psalmist, ' I will take heed to my ways, that I sin not with my tongue. I will keep my mouth with a bridle. I will be dumb with silence. I will hold my peace even from good.'

XIX

JUDGE HATE-GOOD

'Hear, O heads of Jacob, and ye princes of the house of Israel . . .
who hate the good and love the evil.'—*Micah.*

THE portrait of Judge Hate-good in
The Pilgrim's Progress is but a poor
replica, as our artists say, of the portrait of Judge Jeffreys in our English
history books. I am sure you have
often read, with astonishment at Bunyan's literary
power, his wonderful account of the trial of Faithful,
when, as Bunyan says, he was brought forth to his
trial in order to his condemnation. We have the
whole ecclesiastical jurisprudence of Charles and
James Stuart put before us in that single satirical
sentence. But, powerful as Bunyan's whole picture
of Judge Hate-good's court is, it is a tame and a
poor picture compared with what all the historians
tell us of the injustice and cruelty of the court of
Judge Jeffreys. Macaulay's portrait of the Lord
Chief Justice of England for ferocity and fiendishness
beats out of sight Bunyan's picture of that judge
who keeps Satan's own seal in Bunyan's Book.
Jeffreys was bred for his future work at the bar of
the Old Bailey, a bar already proverbial for the
licence of its tongue and for the coarseness of its
cases. Jeffreys served his apprenticeship for the

service that our two last Stuarts had in reserve for him so well, that he soon became, so his beggared biographer describes him, the most consummate bully that ever disgraced an English bench. The boldest impudence when he was a young advocate, and the most brutal ferocity when he was an old judge, sat equally secure on the brazen forehead of George Jeffreys. The real and undoubted ability and scholarship of Jeffreys only made his wickedness the more awful, and his whole career the greater curse both to those whose tool he was, and to those whose blood he drank daily. Jeffreys drank brandy and sang lewd songs all night, and he drank blood and cursed and swore on the bench all day. Just imagine the state of our English courts when a judge could thus assail a poor wretch of a woman after passing a cruel sentence upon her. Hangman,' shouted the ermined brute, 'Hangman, pay particular attention to this lady. Scourge her soundly, man. Scourge her till the blood runs. It is the Christmas season; a cold season for madam to strip in. See, therefore, man, that you warm her shoulders thoroughly.' And you all know who Richard Baxter was. You have all read his seraphic book, *The Saints' Rest.* Well, besides being the Richard Baxter so well known to our saintly fathers and mothers, he was also, and he was emphatically, the peace-maker of the Puritan party. Baxter's political principles were of the most temperate and conciliatory, and indeed, almost royalist kind. He was a man of strong passions, indeed, but all the strength and heat of his passions ran out into his hatred of sin and his love of holiness, and an unsparing and con-

suming care for the souls of his people. Very
Faithful himself stood before the bar of Judge
Jeffreys in the person of Richard Baxter. It took
all the barefaced falsehood and scandalous injustice
of the crown prosecutors to draw out the sham
indictment that was read out in court against inoffensive Richard Baxter. But what was lacking
in the charge of the crown was soon made up by
the abominable scurrility of the judge. 'You are a
schismatical knave,' roared out Jeffreys, as soon as
Baxter was brought into court. 'You are an old
hypocritical villain.' And then, clasping his hands
and turning up his eyes, he sang through his nose :
'O Lord, we are Thy peculiar people : we are Thy
dear and only people.' 'You old blockhead,' he
again roared out, 'I will have you whipped through
the city at the tail of the cart. By the grace of
God I will look after you, Richard.' And the tiger
would have been as good as his word had not an
overpowering sense of shame compelled the other
judges to protest and get Baxter's inhuman sentence
commuted to fine and imprisonment. And so on,
and so on. But it was Jeffreys' 'Western Circuit,'
as it was called, that filled up the cup of his infamy—
an infamy, say the historians, that will last as long
as the language and the history of England last.
The only parallel to it is the infamy of a royal house
and a royal court that could welcome home and
promote to honour such a detestable miscreant as
Jeffreys was. But the slaughter in Somerset was
only over in order that a similar slaughter in London
might begin. Let those who have a stomach for
more blood and tears follow out the hell upon earth

that James Stuart and George Jeffreys together let loose on the best life of England in their now fast-shortening day. Was Judge Jeffreys, some of you will ask me, born and bred in hell? Was the devil his father, and original sin his mother? Or, was he not the very devil himself come to earth for a season in English flesh? No, my brethren, not so. Judge Jeffreys was one of ourselves. Little George Jeffreys was born and brought up in a happy English home. He was baptised and confirmed in an English church. He took honours in an English university. He ate dinners, was called to the bar, conducted cases, and took silk in an English court of justice. And in the ripeness of his years and of his services, he wore the honourable ermine and sat upon the envied wool-sack of an English sovereign. It would have been far less awful and far less alarming to think of, had Judge Jeffreys been, as you supposed, a pure devil let loose on the Church of Christ and the awakening liberty of England. But some innocent soul will ask me next whether there has ever been any other monster on the face of the earth like Judge Jeffreys; and whether by any possibility there are any such monsters anywhere in our own day. Yes, truth compels me to reply. Yes, there are, plenty, too many. Only their environment, nowadays, as our naturalists say, does not permit them to grow to such strength and dimensions as those of James Stuart, and George Jeffreys, his favourite judge. At the same time, be not deceived by your own deceitful heart, nor by any other deceiver's smooth speeches. Judge Jeffreys is in yourself, only circumstances have not yet let him fully show himself in you. Still, if you look close enough and deep enough into your own hearts, you will see the same wicked light glancing sometimes there that used so to terrify Judge Jeffreys' prisoners when they saw it in his wicked eyes. If you lay your ear close enough to your own heart, you will sometimes hear something of that same hiss with which that human serpent sentenced to torture and to death the men and the women who would not submit to his command. The same savage laughter also will sometimes all but escape your lips as you think of how your enemy has been made to suffer in body and in estate. O yes, the very same hell-broth that ran for blood in Judge Jeffreys' heart is in all our hearts also; and those who have the least of its poison left in their hearts will be the foremost to confess its presence, and to hate and condemn and bewail themselves on account of its terrible dregs.

HATE-GOOD is an awful enough name for any human being to bear. Those who really know what goodness is, and then, what hatred is,—they will feel how awful a thing it is for any man to hate goodness. But there is something among us sinful men far more awful than even that, and that is to hate God. The carnal mind, writes the apostle Paul to the Romans—and it is surely the most terrible sentence that often terrible enough apostle ever wrote—the carnal mind is enmity against God. And Dr. John Owen annotating on that sentence is equally terrible. The carnal mind, he says, has 'chosen a great enemy indeed.' And having mentioned John Owen, will you let me once more beseech all students of divinity, that is, all students, amongst other things, of the desperate depravity of the human heart, to read John Owen's sixth volume till they have it by heart,—by a broken, believing heart. Owen *On Indwelling Sin* is one of the greatest works of the great Puritan period. It is a really great, and as we nowadays say, a truly scientific work to the bargain. But all that by the way. Yes, this carnal heart that is still left in every one of us has chosen a great enemy, and it would need both strong and faithful allies in order to fight him. The hatred that His Son also met with when He was in this world is one of the most hateful pages of this hateful world's hateful history. He knew His own heart towards His enemies, and thus He was able to say to the Searcher of Hearts with His dying breath, They hated Me without a cause. Truly our hatred is hottest when it is most unjust.

' Look to yourselves,' wrote the apostle John to the elect lady and her children. Yes ; let us all look sharply and suspiciously to ourselves in this matter now in hand, and we shall not need John Owen nor anybody else to discover to us the hatred and the hatefulness of our own hearts. Look to yourselves, and the work of the law will soon be fulfilled in you. *Homo homini lupus,* taught an old philosopher who had studied moral philosophy not in books so much as in his own heart. ' Is no man naturally good ?' asked innocent Lady Macleod of Dunvegan Castle at her guest, Dr. Samuel Johnson. ' No, madam, no more than a wolf.' That is quite past all question with all those who either in natural morals or in revealed religion look to and know and characterise themselves. We have all an inborn propensity to dislike one another, and a very small provocation will suddenly blow that banked-up furnace into a flame. It is ever present with me, says self-examining Paul, and hence its so sudden and so destructive outbreaks. So the written or the printed name of our enemy, his image in our mind, his passing step, his figure out of the window; his wife, his child, his carriage, his cart in the street, anything, everything will stir up our heart at the man we do not like. And the whole of our so honest Bible, our present text, and the illustrations of our text in Judge Jeffreys' and Judge Hate-good's courts, all go to show that the better a man is the more sometimes will we hate him. Good men, better men than we are, men who in public life and in private life pursue great and good ends, of necessity cross and go counter to us in our pursuit of small, selfish, evil ends, and of necessity we hate them. For, cross a selfish sinner sufficiently and you have a very devil—as many good men, if they knew it, have in us. Again, good men who come into contact with us cannot help seeing our bad lives, our tempers, our selfishness, our public and private vices; and we see that they see us, and we cannot love those whose averted eye so goes to our conscience. And not only in the hatred of good men, but if you know of God how to watch yourselves, you will find yourselves out every day also in the hatred of good movements, good causes, good institutions, and good works. There are doctors who would far rather hear of their rival's patient expiring in his hands than hear their

rival's success trumpeted through all the town.
There are ministers, also, who would rather that
the masses of the city and the country sank yet
deeper into improvidence and drink and neglect
of ordinances than that they were rescued by any
other church than their own. They hate to hear
of the successes of another church. There are party
politicians who would rather that the ship of the
state ran on the rocks both in her home and her
foreign policy than that the opposite party should
steer her amid a nation's cheers into harbour. And
so of good news. I will stake the divine truth of
this evening's Scriptures, and of their historical and
imaginative illustrations, on the feelings, if you
know how to observe, detect, characterise, and
confess them,—the feelings, I say, that will rise in
your heart to-morrow morning when you read what
is good news to other men, even to good men, and
to the families and family interests of good men.
It does not matter one atom into what profession,
office, occupation, interest you track the corrupt
heart of man, as sure as a substance casts a shadow,
so sure will you find your own selfish heart hating
goodness when the goodness does not serve or
flatter you.

Now, though they will never be many, yet there
must be some men among us, one here and another
there, who have so looked at and found out themselves. I can well believe that some men here came
up to this house to-night trembling in their heart
all the way. They felt the very advertisement go
through them like a knife : they felt that they were
summoned up hither almost by name as to judg-

ment. For they feel every day, though they have never told their feelings to any, that they have this horrible heart deep-seated within them to love evil and to hate good. They gnash their teeth at themselves as they catch themselves rejoicing in iniquity. They feel their hearts expanding, and they know that their faces shine, when you tell them evil tidings. They sicken and lose heart and sit solitary when you carry to them a good report. They feel as John Bunyan felt, that no one but the devil can equal them in pollution of heart. And their wonder sometimes is that the Searcher of Hearts does not drive them down where devils dwell and hate God and man and one another. They look around them when the penitential psalm is being sung, and they smile bitterly to themselves. O people of God, they say, you do not know what you are saying. Leave that psalm to me. I can sing it. I can tell to God what He knows about sin, and about sin in the heart. Stand away back from me, that man says, for I am a leper. The chief of sinners is beside you. A whited sepulchre stands open beside you.—Stop now, O hating and hateful man, and let me speak for a single moment before we separate. Before you say any more about yourself, and before you leave the house of God, lift up your broken heart and with all your might bless God that He has opened your eyes and taught you how to look at yourself and how to hate yourself. There are hundreds of honest Christian men and women in this house at this moment to whom God has not done as, in His free grace, He has done to you. For He has not only begun a good work in you, but

He has begun that special and peculiar work which, when it goes on to perfection, makes a great and an eminent saint of God. To know your own heart as you evidently know it, and to hate it as you say you hate it, and to hunger after a clean heart as, with every breath, you hunger,—all that, if you would only believe it, sets you, or will yet set you, high up among the people of God. Be comforted; it is your bounden duty to be comforted. God deserves it at your hands that you be more than comforted amid such unmistakable signs of His eminent grace to you. And be patient under your exceptional sanctification. Rome was not built in a day. You cannot reverse the awful law of your sanctification. You cannot be saved by Jesus Christ and His Holy Spirit without seeing yourself, and you cannot see yourself without hating yourself, and you cannot begin to hate yourself without all your hatred henceforth turning against yourself. You are deep in the red-hot bosom of the refiner's fire. And when you are once sufficiently tried by the Divine Refiner of Souls, He will in His own good time and way bring you out as gold. Be patient, therefore, till the coming of the Lord. And say continually amid all your increasing knowledge of yourself, and amid all your increasing hatred of yourself, ' As for me, I will behold Thy face in righteousness; I shall be satisfied when I awake with Thy likeness.'

XX

FAITHFUL IN VANITY FAIR[1]

'Be thou faithful.'—*Rev.* ii. 10.

THE breadth of John Bunyan's mind, the largeness of his heart, and the tolerance of his temper all come excellently out in his fine portrait of Faithful. New beginners in personal religion, when they first take up *The Pilgrim's Progress* in earnest, always try to find out something in themselves that shall somewhat correspond to the recorded experience of Christian, the chief pilgrim. And they are afraid that all is not right with them unless they, like him, have had, to begin with, a heavy burden on their back. They look for something in their religious life that shall answer to the Slough of Despond also, to the Hill Difficulty, to the House Beautiful, and, especially and indispensably, to the place somewhat ascending with a cross upon it and an open sepulchre beneath it. And because they cannot always find all these things in themselves in the exact order and in the full power in which they are told of Christian in Bunyan's book, they begin to have doubts about themselves as to whether they are true pilgrims at all. But

[1] Delivered June 26th, 1892, on the eve of a general election.

here is Faithful, with whom Christian held such
sweet and confidential discourse, and yet he had
come through not a single one of all these things.
The two pilgrims had come from the same City of
Destruction indeed, and they had met at the gate
of Vanity and passed through Vanity Fair together,
but, till they embraced one another again in the
Celestial City, that was absolutely all the experience
they had in common. Faithful had never had any
such burden on his back as that was which had for
so long crushed Christian to the earth. And the
all but complete absence of such a burden may have
helped to let Faithful get over the Slough of
Despond dry shod. He had the good lot to escape
Sinai also and the Hill Difficulty, and his passing by
the House Beautiful and not making the acquaintance of Discretion and Prudence and Charity may
have had something to do with the fact that one
named Wanton had like to have done him such a
mischief. His remarkable experiences, however,
with Adam the First, with Moses, and then with
the Man with holes in His hands, all that makes
up a page in Faithful's autobiography we could ill
have spared. His encounter with Shame also, and
soon afterwards with Talkative, are classical passages
in his so individual history. Altogether, it would be
almost impossible for us to imagine two pilgrims
talking so heartily together, and yet so completely
unlike one another. A very important lesson surely
as to how we should abstain from measuring other
men by ourselves, as well as ourselves by other
men; an excellent lesson also as to how we should
learn to allow for all possible varieties among good

men, both in their opinions, their experiences, and their attainments. True Puritan as the author of *The Pilgrim's Progress* is, he is no Procrustes. He does not cut down all his pilgrims to one size, nor does he clip them all into one pattern. They are all thinking men, but they are not all men of one way of thinking. John Bunyan is as fresh as Nature herself, and as free and full as Holy Scripture herself in the variety, in the individuality, and even in the idiosyncrasy of his spiritual portrait gallery.

Vanity Fair is one of John Bunyan's universally-admitted masterpieces. The very name of the fair is one of his happiest strokes. Thackeray's famous book owes half its popularity to the happy name he borrowed from John Bunyan. Thackeray's author's heart must have leaped in his bosom when Vanity Fair struck him as a title for his great satire. 'Then I saw in my dream that when they were got out of the wilderness they presently saw a town before them, and the name of that town is Vanity, and at that town there is a fair, kept called Vanity Fair. The fair is kept all the year long, and it beareth the name of Vanity Fair, because the town where it is kept is lighter than Vanity. And, also, because all that is sold there is vanity. As is the saying of the wise, All that cometh is vanity. The fair is no new erected business, but a thing of ancient standing : I will show you the original of it. About five thousand years ago there were pilgrims walking to the Celestial City, as these two honest persons now are, and Beelzebub, Apollyon, and Legion, with their companions, perceiving that by the path that the pilgrims made, that their way to the city lay through this town of Vanity, they contrived there to set up a fair: a fair wherein should be sold all sorts of vanity, and that it should last all the year long. Therefore at this fair are all such merchandise sold as houses, lands, trades, places, honours, preferments, titles, countries, kingdoms, pleasures, and delights of all sorts, as wives, husbands, children, masters, servants, lives, blood, bodies, souls, silver, gold, precious stones, and what not. And, moreover, at this fair at all times there is to be seen juggling, cheats, games, plays, fools, apes, knaves, and rogues, and that of every kind.' And then our author goes on to tell us the names of the various streets and rows where such and such wares are vended. And from that again he goes on to tell how the Prince of princes Himself went at one time through this same fair, and that upon a fair day too, and how the lord of the fair himself came and took Him from street to street to try to get Him induced to cheapen and buy some of the vain merchandise. But as it turned out He had no mind to the merchandise in question, and He therefore passed through the town without laying out so much as one farthing upon its vanities. The fair, therefore, you will see, is of long standing and a very great fair. Now, our two pilgrims had heard of all that, they remembered also what Evangelist had told them about the fair, and so they buttoned up their pockets and pushed through the booths in the hope of getting out at the upper gate before any one had time to speak to them. But that was not possible, for they were soon set upon by the men of the fair, who cried after them: ' Hail, strangers, look here, what will you buy?' 'We buy the truth only,' said Faithful, 'and we do not see any of that article of merchandise set out on any of your stalls. And from that began a hubbub that ended in a riot, and the riot in the apprehension and shutting up in a public cage of the two innocent pilgrims. Lord Hate-good was the judge on the bench of Vanity in the day of their trial, and the three witnesses who appeared in the witness-box against the two prisoners were Envy, Superstition, and Pickthank. The twelve jurymen who sat on their case were Mr. Blindman, Mr. No-good, Mr. Malice, Mr. Love-lust, Mr. Live-loose, Mr. Heady, Mr. High-mind, Mr. Enmity, Mr. Liar, Mr. Cruelty, Mr. Hate-light, and Mr. Implacable,—Mr. Blindman to be the foreman. And it was before these men that Faithful was brought forth to his trial in order to his condemnation. And very soon after his trial Faithful came to his end. 'Now I saw that there stood behind the multitude a chariot and a couple of horses waiting for Faithful, who (so soon as his adversaries had despatched him) was taken up into it, and straightway was carried up through the clouds, with sound of trumpet, the nearest way to the Celestial gate.'

Now, I cannot tell you how it was, I cannot account for it to myself, but it is nevertheless absolutely true that as I was reading my author last week and was meditating my present exposition, it came somehow into my mind, and I could not get it out of my mind, that there is a great and a close similarity between John Bunyan's Vanity Fair and a general election. And, all I could do

to keep the whole thing out of my mind, one similarity after another would leap up into my mind and
would not be put out of it. I protest that I did
not go out to seek for such similarities, but the
more I frowned on them the thicker they came.
And then the further question arose as to whether
I should write them down or no; and then much
more, as to whether I should set them out before
my people or no. As you will easily believe, I was
immediately in a real strait as to what I should do.
I saw on the one side what would be sure to be
said by ill-natured people and people of a hasty
judgment. And I saw with much more anxiety
what would be felt even when they restrained
themselves from saying it by timid and cautious
and scrupulous people. I had the full fear of all
such judges before my eyes; but, somehow, something kept this before my eyes also, that, as Evangelist met the two pilgrims just as they were
entering the fair, so, for anything I knew to the
contrary, it might be of God, that I also, in my own
way, should warn my people of the real and special
danger that their souls will be in for the next fortnight. And as I thought of it a procession of
people passed before me all bearing to this day the
stains and scars they had taken on their hearts and
their lives and their characters at former general
elections. And, like Evangelist, I felt a divine
desire taking possession of me to do all I could to
pull my people out of gun-shot of the devil at this
election. And, then, when I read again how both
the pilgrims thanked Evangelist for his exhortation,
and told him withal that they would have him speak

further to them about the dangers of the way, I said at last to myself, that the thanks of one true Christian saved in anything and in any measure from the gun of the devil are far more to be attended to by a minister than the blame and the neglect of a hundred who do not know their hour of temptation and will not be told it. And so I took my pen and set down some similarities between Vanity Fair and the approaching election, with some lessons to those who are not altogether beyond being taught.

Well, then, in the first place, the only way to the Celestial City ran through Vanity Fair; by no possibility could the advancing pilgrims escape the temptations and the dangers of the fatal fair. He that will go to the Celestial City and yet not go through Vanity Fair must needs go out of the world. And so it is with the temptations and trials of the next ten days. We cannot get past them. They are laid down right across our way. And to many men now in this house the next ten days will be a time of simply terrible temptation. If I had been quite sure that all my people saw that and felt that, I would not have introduced here to-night what some of them, judging too hastily, will certainly call this so secular and unseemly subject. But I am so afraid that many not untrue, and in other things most earnest men amongst us, do not yet know sufficiently the weakness and the evil of their own hearts, that I wish much, if they will allow me, to put them on their guard. ''Tis hard,' said Contrite, who was a householder and had a vote in the town of Vanity, ''tis hard keeping our hearts and our spirits in any good order when we are in a cumbered condition. And you may be sure that we are full of hurry at fair-time. He that lives in such a place as this is, and that has to do with such as we have to do with, has need of an item to caution him to take heed every hour of the day.' Now, if all my people, and all this day's communicants, were only contrite enough, I would leave them to the hurry of the approaching election with much more comfort. But as it is, I wish to give them such an item as I am able to caution them for the next ten days. Let them know, then, that their way for the next fortnight lies, I will not say through a fair of jugglings and cheatings, carried on by apes and knaves, but, to speak without figure, their way certainly lies through what will be to many of them a season of the greatest temptation to the very worst of all possible sins—to anger and bitterness and ill-will; to no end of evil-thinking and evil-speaking; to the breaking up of life-long friendships; and to widespread and lasting damage to the cause of Christ, which is the cause of truth and love, meekness and a heavenly mind. Now, amid all that, as Evangelist said to the two pilgrims, look well to your own hearts. Let none of all these evil things enter your heart from the outside, and let none of all these evil things come out of your hearts from the inside. Set your faces like a flint from the beginning against all evil-speaking and evil-thinking. Let your own election to the kingdom of heaven be always before you, and walk worthy of it; and amid all the hurry of things seen and temporal, believe steadfastly concerning the things that are eternal, and walk worthy of them.

'We buy the truth and we sell it not again for anything,' was the reply of the two pilgrims to every stall-keeper as they passed up the fair, and this it was that made them to be so hated and hunted down by the men of the fair. And, in like manner, there is nothing more difficult to get hold of at an election time than just the very truth. All the truth on any question is not very likely to be found put forward in the programme of any man or any party, and, even if it were, a general election is not the best time for you to find it out. 'I design the search after truth to be the one business of my life,' wrote the future Bishop Butler at the age of twenty-one. And whether you are to be a member of Parliament or a silent voter for a member of Parliament, you, too, must love truth and search for her as for hid treasure from your youth up. You must search for all kinds of truth,—historical, political, scientific, and religious,—with much reading, much observation, and much reflection. And those who have searched longest and dug deepest will always be found to be the most temperate, patient, and forbearing with those who have not yet found the truth. I do not know who first said it, but he was a true disciple of Socrates and Plato who first said it. 'Plato,' he said, 'is my friend, and Socrates is my friend, but the truth is much more my friend.' There is a thrill of enthusiasm, admiration and hope that goes through the whole country and comes down out of history as often as we hear or read of some public man parting with all

his own past, as well as with all his leaders and
patrons and allies and colleagues in the present,
and taking his solitary way out after the truth.
Many may call that man Quixotic, visionary, un-
practical, imprudent, and he may be all that and
more, but to follow conscience and the love of
truth even when they are for the time leading him
wrong is noble, and is every way far better both for
himself and for the cause he serves, than if he were
always found following his leaders loyally and even
walking in the way of righteousness with the love of
self and the love of party at bottom ruling his heart.
How healthful and how refreshing at an election
time it is to hear a speech replete with the love of
the truth, full knowledge of the subject, and with the
dignity, the good temper, the respect for opponents,
and the love of fair play that full knowledge of the
whole subject is so well fitted to bring with it!
And next to hearing such a speaker is the pleasure
of meeting such a hearer or such a reader at such a
time.   Now, I want such readers and such hearers,
if not such speakers, to be found all the next fortnight among my office-bearers and my people.   Be
sure you say to some of your political opponents
something like this:—' I do not profess to read all the
speeches that fill the papers at present.   I do not
read all the utterances made even on my own side,
and much less all the utterances made on your side.
But there is one of your speakers I always read,
and I almost always find him instructive and
impressive, a gentleman, if not a Christian.   He is
fair, temperate, frank, bold, and independent ; and,
to my mind at least, he always throws light on these

so perplexing questions.' Now, if you have the intelligence and the integrity and the fair-mindedness to say something like that to a member of the opposite party you have poured oil on the waters of party; nay, you are in that a wily politician, for you have almost, just in saying that, won over your friend to your own side. So noble is the love of truth, and so potent is the high-principled pursuit and the fearless proclamation of the truth.

A general election is a trying time to all kinds of public men, but it is perhaps most trying of all to Christian ministers. Unless they are to disfranchise themselves and are to detach and shut themselves in from all interest in public affairs altogether, an election time is to our ministers, beyond any other class of citizens perhaps, a peculiarly trying time. How they are to escape the Scylla of cowardice and the contempt of all free and true men on the one hand, and the Charybdis of pride and self-will and scorn of other men's opinions and wishes on the other, is no easy dilemma to our ministers. Some happily constituted and happily circumstanced ministers manage to get through life, and even through political life, without taking or giving a wound in all their way. They are so wise and so watchful; they are so inoffensive, unprovoking, and conciliatory; and even where they are not always all that, they have around them sometimes a people who are so patient and tolerant and full of the old-fashioned respect for their minister that they do not attempt to interfere with him. Then, again, some ministers preach so well, and perform all their pastoral work so well, that they make it unsafe and

impossible for the most censorious and intolerant of
their people to find fault with them. But all our
ministers are not like that. And all our congregations are not like that. And those of our ministers
who are not like that must just be left to bear that
which their past unwisdom or misfortune has brought
upon them. Only, if they have profited by their
past mistakes or misfortunes, a means of grace, and
an opportunity of better playing the man is again
at their doors. I am sure you will all join with me
in the prayer that all our ministers, as well as all
their people, may come well out of the approaching
election.

There is yet one other class of public men, if I
may call them so, many of whom come almost worse
out of an election time than even our ministers, and
that class is composed of those, who, to continue
the language of Vanity Fair, keep the cages of the
fair. I wish I had to-night, what I have not, the
ear of the conductors of our public journals. For,
what an omnipotence in God's providence to this
generation for good or evil is theirs! If they
would only all consider well at election times, and
at all times, who they put into their cages and for
what reason; if they would only all ask what can
that man's motives be for throwing such dirt at his
neighbour; if they would only all set aside all the
letters they will get during the next fortnight that
are avowedly composed on the old principle of
calumniating boldly in the certainty that some of it
will stick, what a service they would do to the cause
of love and truth and justice, which is, surely, after
all, their own cause also! The very best papers sin

sadly in this respect when their conductors are full for the time of party passion. And it is inexpressibly sad when a reader sees great journals to which he owes a lifelong debt of gratitude absolutely poisoned under his very eyes with the malignant spirit of untruthful partisanship. But so long as our public cages are so kept, let those who are exposed in them resolve to imitate Christian and Faithful, who behaved themselves amid all their ill-usage yet more wisely, and received all the ignominy and shame that was cast upon them with so much meekness and patience that it actually won to their side several of the men of the fair.

My brethren, this is the last time this season that I shall be able to speak to you from this pulpit; and, perhaps, the last time altogether. But, if it so turns out, I shall not repent that the last time I spoke to you, and that, too, immediately after the communion table, the burden of my message was the burden of my Master's message after the first communion table. 'If ye know these things, happy are ye if ye do them. A new commandment I give unto you, that ye love one another. By this shall all men know that ye are My disciples, if ye have love one to another. Herein is My Father glorified, that ye bear much fruit, so shall ye be My disciples. These things have I spoken unto you that in Me ye might have peace. In the world ye shall have tribulation; but be of good cheer, I have overcome the world. Know ye what I have done unto you? Ye call Me Master and Lord, and ye say well, for so I am.'

XXI

BY-ENDS

'Ye seek Me, not because ye saw the miracles, but because ye did eat of the loaves.'—*Our Lord.*

N no part of John Bunyan's ingenious book is his strong sense and his sarcastic and humorous vein better displayed than just in his description of By-ends, and in the full and particular account he gives of the kinsfolk and affinity of By-ends. Is there another single stroke in all sacred literature better fitted at once to teach the gayest and to make the gravest smile than just John Bunyan's sketch of By-ends' great-grandfather, the founder of the egoistical family of Fairspeech, who was, to begin with, but a waterman who always looked one way and rowed another? By-ends' wife also is a true helpmate to her husband. She was my Lady Feigning's favourite daughter, under whose nurture and example the young lady had early come to a quite extraordinary pitch of good breeding; and now that she was a married woman, she and her husband had, so their biographer tells us, two firm points of family religion in which they were always agreed and according to which they brought up all their children, namely, never to strive too much against wind and tide, and always to watch when

Religion was walking on the sunny side of the street in his silver slippers, and then at once to cross over and take his arm. But abundantly amusing and entertaining as John Bunyan is at the expense of By-ends and his family and friends, he has far other aims in view than the amusement and entertainment of his readers. Bunyan uses all his great gifts of insight and sense and humour and scorn so as to mark unmistakably the road and to guide the progress of his reader's soul to God, his chiefest end and his everlasting portion.

It was no small part of our Lord's life of humiliation on the earth,—much more so than His being born in a low condition and being made under the law, —to have to go about all His days among men, knowing in every case and on every occasion what was in man. It was a real humiliation to our Lord to see those watermen of the sea of Tiberias sweating at their oars as they rowed round and round the lake after Him; and His humiliation came still more home to Him as often as He saw His own disciples disputing and pressing who should get closest to Him while for a short season He walked in the sunshine; just as it was His estate of exaltation already begun, when He could enter into Himself and see to the bottom of His own heart, till He was able to say that it was His very meat and drink to do His father's will, and to finish the work His Father had given Him to do. The men of Capernaum went out after our Lord in their boats because they had eaten of the multiplied loaves and hoped to do so again. Zebedee's children had forsaken all and followed our Lord, because they counted to sit the one on His right hand and the other on His left hand in His soon-coming kingdom. The pain and the shame all that cost our Lord, we can only remotely imagine. But as for Himself, our Lord never once had to blush in secret at His own motives. He never once had to hang down His head at the discovery of His own selfish aims and by-ends. Happy man! The thought of what He should eat or what He should drink, or wherewithal He should be clothed never troubled His head. The thought of success, as His poor-spirited disciples counted success, the thought of honour and power and praise, never once rose in His heart. All these things, and all things like them, had no attraction for Him; they awoke nothing but indifference and contempt in Him. But to please His Father, and to hear from time to time His Father's voice saying that He was well pleased with His beloved Son,—that was better than life to our Lord. To find out and follow every new day His Father's mind and will, and to finish every night another part of His Father's appointed work,—that was more than His necessary food to our Lord. The great schoolmen, as they meditated on these deep matters, had a saying to the effect that all created things take their true goodness or their true evil from the end they aim at. And thus it was that our Lord, aiming only at His Father's ends and never at His own, both manifested and attained to a Divine goodness, just as the greedy crowds of Galilee and the disputatious disciples, as long and as far as they made their belly or their honour their end and aim, to that extent fell short of all true goodness, all true satisfaction, and all true acceptance.

By-ends was so called because he was full of low, mean, selfish motives, and of nothing else. All that this wretched creature did, he did with a single eye to himself. The best things that he did became bad things in his self-seeking hands. His very religion stank in those men's nostrils who knew what was in his heart. By-ends was one of our Lord's whited sepulchres. And so deep, so pervading, and so abiding is this corrupt taint in human nature, that long after a man has had his attention called to it, and is far on to a clean escape from it, he still —nay, he all the more—languishes and faints and is ready to die under it. Just hear what two great servants of God have said on this humiliating and degrading matter. Writing on this subject with all his wonted depth and solemnity, Hooker says, 'Even in the good things that we do, how many defects are there intermingled! For God in that which is done respecteth especially the mind and intention of the doer. Cut off, then, all those things wherein we have regarded our own glory, those things which we do to please men, or to satisfy our own liking, those things which we do with any by-respect, and not sincerely and purely for the love of God, and a small score will serve for the number of our righteous deeds. Let the holiest and best things we do be considered. We are never better affected to God than when we pray; yet, when we pray, how are our affections many times distracted! How little reverence do we show to that God unto whom we speak! How little remorse of our own miseries!

How little taste of the sweet influence of His tender mercy do we feel! The little fruit we have in holiness, it is, God knoweth, corrupt and unsound; we put no confidence at all in it, we challenge nothing in the world for it, we dare not call God to a reckoning as if we had Him in our debt-books; our continued suit to Him is, and must be, to bear with our infirmities, and to pardon our offences.' And Thomas Shepard, a divine of a very different school, as we say, but a saint and a scholar equal to the best, and indeed with few to equal him, thus writes in his *Spiritual Experiences* :—' On Sabbath morning I saw that I had a secret eye to my own name in all that I did, for which I judged myself worthy of death. On another Sabbath, when I came home, I saw the deep hypocrisy of my heart, that in my ministry I sought to comfort and quicken others, that the glory might reflect on me as well as on God. On the evening before the sacrament I saw that mine own ends were to procure honour, pleasure, gain to myself, and not to the Lord, and I saw how impossible it was for me to seek the Lord for Himself, and to lay up all my honour and all my pleasures in Him. On Sabbath-day, when the Lord had given me some comfortable enlargements, I searched my heart and found my sin. I saw that though I did to some extent seek Christ's glory, yet I sought it not alone, but my own glory too. After my Wednesday sermon I saw the pride of my heart acting thus, that presently my ·heart would look out and ask whether I had done well or ill. Hereupon I saw my vileness to make men's opinions my rule. The Lord thus gave me some

glimpse of myself, and a good day that was to me.'
One would think that this was By-ends himself
climbed up into the ministry. And so it was. And
yet David Brainerd could write on his deathbed
about Thomas Shepard in this way. ' He valued
nothing in religion that was not done to the glory
of God, and, oh! that others would lay the stress of
religion here also. His method of examining his
ends and aims and the temper of his mind both
before and after preaching, is an excellent example
for all who bear the sacred character. By this
means they are like to gain a large acquaintance
with their own hearts, as it is evident he had with
his.'

But it is not those who bear the sacred character
of the ministry alone who are full of by-ends. We
all are. You all are. And there is not one all-
reaching, all-exposing, and all-humbling way of
salvation appointed for ministers, and another, a
more external, superficial, easy, and self-satisfied
way for their people. No. Not only must the
ambitious and disputing disciples enter into themselves and become witnesses and judges and exe-
cutioners within themselves before they can be
saved or be of any use in the salvation of others—
not only they, but the fishermen of the Lake of
Tiberias, they also must open their hearts to these
stabbing words of Christ, and see how true it is
that they had followed Him for loaves and fishes,
and not for His grace and His truth. And only
when they had seen and submitted to that humiliating self-discovery would their true acquaintance
with Christ and their true search after Him begin.

Come, then, all my brethren, and not ministers only, waken up to the tremendous importance of that which you have utterly neglected, it may be ostentatiously neglected, up to this hour,—the true nature, the true character, of your motives and your ends. Enter into yourselves. Be not strangers and foreigners to yourselves. Let not the day of judgment be any surprise to you. Witness against, judge, and execute yourselves, and that especially because of your by-aims and by-ends. Take up the touchstone of truth and lay it upon your most secret heart. Do not be afraid to discover how double-minded and deceitful your heart is. Hunt your heart down. Track it to its most secret lair. Put its true name, and continue to put its true name, upon the main motive of your life. Extort an answer by boot and by wheel, only extort an answer from the inner man of the heart, to the torturing question as to what is his treasure, his hope, his deepest wish, his daily dream. Watch not against any outward enemy, keep all your eyes and all your ears to your own thoughts. God keeps His awful eye on your thoughts. His eye goes at every glance to that great depth in you. Even His all-seeing eye can go no deeper into you than to your secret thoughts. Go you as deep as God goes, and you will be a wise man; go as deep and as often as He does, and then you will soon come to see eye to eye with God, not only about your own thoughts, but about His thoughts too, and about everything else. Till you begin to watch your own thoughts, and to watch them especially in their aims and their ends, you will have no idea what that moral and spiritual life is that all God's saints live; that life that Christ lived, and which He this night summons you all to enter henceforth upon.

It is such a happy fact that it cannot be too often told, that in the things of the soul really and truly to know and feel the disease is to have already entered on the remedy. You will not feel, indeed, that you have entered on the remedy; but that does not much matter so long as you really have. And there is nothing more certain among all the certainties of divine things than that he who feels himself to be in death and hell with his heart so full of by-ends is all the time as far from death and hell as any one can be who is still on this side of heaven. When a man's whole will and desire is set on God, as is now and then the case, that man is perilously near a sudden and an abundant entrance into that life and that presence where his heart has for so long been. When a man is half mad with his own heart, as Thomas Shepard for one was, that stranger on the earth is at last within a step of that happy coast where all wishes end. Watch that man. Take a last look at that man. He will soon be taken out of your sight. Ere ever he is himself aware, he will be rapt up into that life where saints and angels seek not their own will, labour not for their own profit or promotion, listen not for their own praises, but find their blessedness, the half of which had not here been told them, in glorifying God and in enjoying Him for ever.

You must all have heard the name of a book that has helped many a saint now in glory to the examination and the keeping of his own heart. I

refer to Jeremy Taylor's *Holy Living and Dying.*
Take two or three of Taylor's excellent rules with
you as you go down from God's house to-night.
'If you would really live a holy life and die a holy
death,' says Taylor, 'learn to reflect in your every
action on your secret end in it ; consider with yourself why you do it, and what you propound to
yourself for your reward. Pray importunately that
all your purposes and all your motives may be
sanctified. Renew and rekindle your purest purposes by such ejaculations as these : " Not unto us,
O God, not unto us, but to Thy name be all the
praise. I am in this Thy servant ; let all the gain
be Thine." In great and eminent actions let there
be a special and peculiar act of resignation or
oblation made to God ; and in smaller and more
frequent actions fail not to secure a pious habitual
intention.' And so on. And above all, I will
add, labour and pray till you feel in your heart
that you love God with a supreme and an ever-
growing love. And, far as that may be above you
as yet, impress your heart with the assurance that
such a love is possible to you also, and that you
can never be safe or happy till you attain to that
love. Other men once as far from the supreme
love of God as you are have afterwards attained to
it ; and so will you if you continue to set it before
yourself. Think often on God ; read the best books
about God ; call continually upon God ; hold an
intimate communion with God, till you feel that
you also actually and certainly love God. And
though you begin with loving God because He first
loved you, you will, beginning with that, rise far

above that till you come to love Him for what He is in Himself as well as for what He has done for you. 'I have done this in order to have a seat in the Academy,' said a young man, handing the solution of a problem to an old philosopher. 'Sir,' was the reply, 'with such dispositions you will never earn a seat there. Science must be loved for its own sake, and not for any advantage to be derived from it.' And much more is that true of the highest of all the sciences, the knowledge and the love of God. Love Him, then, till you arrive at loving Him for Himself, and then you shall be for ever delivered from all self-love and by-ends, and shall both glorify and enjoy God for ever. As all they now do who engaged their hearts on earth to the service and the love and the enjoyment of God is such psalms and prayers as these: 'Whom have I in heaven but Thee? and there is no one on earth that I desire beside Thee. How excellent is Thy loving-kindness, O God! The children of men shall put their trust under the shadow of Thy wings. For with Thee is the fountain of life, and in Thy light shall we see light. As for me, I will behold Thy face in righteousness: I shall be satisfied when I awake with Thy likeness. Thou wilt show me the path of life; in Thy presence is fulness of joy, and at Thy right hand there are pleasures for evermore.'

224

XXII

GIANT DESPAIR

'A wounded spirit who can bear?' —*Solomon.*

EVERY schoolboy has Giant Despair by
heart. The rough road after the
meadow of lilies, the stile into By-
Path-Meadow, the night coming on,
the thunder and the lightning and
the waters rising amain, Giant Despair's apprehension of Christian and Hopeful, their dreadful bed
in his dungeon from Wednesday morning till
Saturday night, how they were famished with
hunger and beaten with a grievous crab-tree cudgel
till they were not able to turn, with many other
sufferings too many and too terrible to be told
which they endured till Saturday about midnight,
when they began to pray, and continued in prayer
till almost break of day;—John Bunyan is surely
the best story-teller in all the world. And, then,
over and above that, as often as a boy reads Giant
Despair and his dungeon to his father and mother,
the two hearers are like Christian and Hopeful when
the Delectable shepherds showed them what had
happened to some who once went in at By-Path stile:
the two pilgrims looked one upon another with tears
gushing out, but yet said nothing to the shepherds.

John Bunyan's own experience enters deeply

into these terrible pages. In composing these terrible pages, Bunyan writes straight and bold out of his own heart and conscience. The black and bitter essence of a whole black and bitter volume is crushed into these four or five bitter pages. Last week I went over *Grace Abounding* again, and marked the passages in which its author describes his own experiences of doubt, diffidence, and despair, till I gave over counting the passages, they are so many. I had intended to illustrate the passage before us to-night out of the kindred materials that I knew were so abundant in Bunyan's terrible autobiography, but I had to give up that idea. It would have taken two or three lectures to itself to tell all that Bunyan suffered all his life long from an easily-wounded spirit. The whole book is just Giant Despair and his dungeon, with a gleam here and there of that sunshiny weather that threw the giant into one of his fits, in which he always lost for the time the use of his limbs. Return often, my brethren, to that masterpiece, *Grace Abounding to the Chief of Sinners*. I have read it a hundred times, but last week it was as fresh and powerful and consoling as ever to my sin-wounded spirit.

Let me select some of the incidents that offer occasion for a comment or two.

1. And, in the first place, take notice, and lay well to heart, how sudden, and almost instantaneous, is the fall of Christian and Hopeful from the very gate of heaven to the very gate of hell. All the Sabbath and the Monday and the Tuesday before that fatal Wednesday, the two pilgrims had walked

with great delight on the banks of a very pleasant river; that river, in fact, which David the King called the river of God, and John, the river of the water of life. They drank also of the water of the river, which was pleasant and enlivening to their weary spirits. On either side of the river was there a meadow curiously beautified with lilies, and it was green all the year long. In this meadow they lay down and slept, for here they might lie down and sleep safely. When they awoke they gathered again of the fruits of the trees, and drank again of the water of the river, and then lay down again to sleep. Thus they did several days and nights. Now, could you have believed it that two such men as our pilgrims were could be in the enjoyment of all that the first half of the week, and then by their own doing should be in Giant Despair's deepest dungeon before the end of the same week? And yet so it was. And all that is written for the solemn warning of those who are at any time in great enlargement and refreshment and joy in their spiritual life. It is intended for all those who are at any time revelling in a season of revival: those, for example, who are just come home from Keswick or Dunblane, as well as for all those who at home have just made the discovery of some great master of the spiritual life, and who are almost beside themselves with their delight in their divine author. If they are new beginners they will not take this warning well, nor will even all old pilgrims lay it aright to heart; but there it is as plain as the plainest, simplest, and most practical writer in our language could put it.

> Behold ye how these crystal streams do glide
> To comfort pilgrims by the highway side;
> The meadows green, besides their fragrant smell,
> Yield dainties for them: And he that can tell
> What pleasant fruits, yea leaves, these trees do yield,
> Will soon sell all that he may buy this field.

Thus the two pilgrims sang: only, adds our author in a parenthesis, they were not, as yet, at their journey's end.

2. 'Now, I beheld in my dream that they had not journeyed far when the river and the way for a time parted. At which the two pilgrims were not a little sorry.' The two pilgrims could not perhaps be expected to break forth into dancing and singing at the parting of the river and the way, even though they had recollected at that moment what the brother of the Lord says about our counting it all joy when we fall into divers temptations. But it would not have been too much to expect from such experienced pilgrims as they by this time were, that they should have suspected and checked and commanded their sorrow. They should have said something like this to one another: Well, it would have been very pleasant had it been our King's will and way with us that we should have finished the rest of our pilgrimage among the apples and the lilies and on the soft and fragrant bank of the river; but we believe that it must in some as yet hidden way be better for us that the river and our road should part from one another at least for a season. Come, brother, and let us go on till we find out our Master's deep and loving mind. But, instead of saying that, Christian and Hopeful soon became like the children of Israel as they journeyed from Mount

Hor, their soul was much discouraged because of the way. And always as they went on they wished for a softer and a better way. And it was so that they very soon came to the very thing they so much wished for. For, what is that on the left hand of the hard road but a stile, and over the stile a meadow as soft to the feet as the meadow of lilies itself? ''Tis just according to my wish,' said Christian; 'here is the easiest going. Come, good Hopeful, and let us go over.' Hopeful: 'But how if the path should lead us out of the way?' 'That's not like,' said the other; 'look, doth it not go along by the wayside?' So Hopeful, being persuaded by his fellow, went after him over the stile.

Call to mind, all you who are delivered and re-stored pilgrims, that same stile that once seduced you. To keep that stile ever before you is at once a safe and a seemly occupation of mind for any one who has made your mistakes and come through your chastisements. Christian's eyes all his after-days filled with tears, and he turned away his face and blushed scarlet, as often as he suddenly came upon any opening in a wall at all like that opening he here persuaded Hopeful to climb through. It is too much to expect that those who are just mounting the stile, and have just caught sight of the smooth path beyond it, will let themselves be pulled back into the hard and narrow way by any persuasion of ours. Christian put down Hopeful's objection till Hopeful broke out bitterly when the thunder was roaring over his head and he was wading about among the dark waters: 'Oh that I had kept myself in my way!' Are you a little sorry to-night that the river and the way are parting in your life? Is your soul discouraged in you because of the soreness of the way? And as you go do you still wish for some better way than the strait way? And have you just espied a stile on the left hand of your narrow and flinty path, and on looking over it is there a pleasant meadow? And does your companion point out to your satisfaction, and, almost to your good conscience, that the soft road runs right along the hard road, only over the stile and outside the fence? Then, good-bye. For it is all over with you. We shall meet you again, please God; but when we meet you again, your mind and memory will be full of shame and remorse and suffering enough to keep you in songs of repentance for all the rest of your life on earth. Farewell!

> The Pilgrims now, to gratify the flesh,
> Will seek its ease; but oh! how they afresh
> Do thereby plunge themselves new grieves into:
> Who seek to please the flesh themselves undo.

3. The two transgressors had not gone far on their own way when night came on and with the night a very great darkness. But what soon added to the horror of their condition was that they heard a man fall into a deep pit right before them, and it sounded to them as if he was dashed to pieces by his fall. So they called to know the matter, but there was none to answer, only they heard a groaning. Then said Hopeful: Where are we now? Then was his fellow silent, as mistrusting that he had led Hopeful out of the way. Now, all that also is true to the very life, and has been taken down by Bunyan from the very life. We have all heard men

falling and heard them groaning just a little before us after we had left the strait road. They had just gone a little farther wrong than we had as yet gone,—just a very little farther; in some cases, indeed, not so far, when they fell and were dashed to pieces with their fall. It was well for us at that dreadful moment that we heard the same voice saying to us for our encouragement as said to the two trembling transgressors: 'Let thine heart be toward the highway, even the way that thou wentest; turn again.' Now, what is it in which you are at this moment going off the right road? What is that life of disobedience or self-indulgence that you are just entering on? Keep your ears open and you will hear hundreds of men and women falling and being dashed to pieces before you and all around you. Are you falling of late too much under the power of your bodily appetites? It is not one man, nor two, well known to you, who have fallen never to rise again out of that horrible pit. Are you well enough aware that you are being led into bad company? Or, is your companion, who is not a bad man in anything else, leading you, in this and in that, into what at any rate is bad for you? You will soon, unless you cut off your companion like a right hand, be found saying with misguided and overruled Hopeful: Oh that I had kept me to my right way! And so on in all manner of sin and trespass. Those who have ears to hear such things hear every day one man after another falling through lust or pride or malice or idleness or in-fidelity, till there is none to answer.

4. 'All hope abandon' was the writing that Dante

read over the door of hell. And the two prisoners
all but abandoned all hope when they found themselves in Giant Despair's dungeon. Only, Christian,
the elder man, had the most distress because their
being where they now were lay mostly at his door.
All this part of the history also is written in Bunyan's
very heart's blood. 'I found it hard work,' he tells
us of himself, 'to pray to God because despair was
swallowing me up. I thought I was as with a
tempest driven away from God. About this time I
did light on that dreadful story of that miserable
mortal, Francis Spira, a book that was to my troubled
spirit as salt when rubbed into a fresh wound; every
groan of that man with all the rest of his actions in
his dolours, as his tears, his prayers, his gnashing of
teeth, his wringing of hands, was as knives and
daggers in my soul, especially that sentence of his
was frightful to me: "Man knows the beginning of
sin, but who bounds the issues thereof?"' We never
read anything like Spira's experience and *Grace
Abounding* and Giant Despair's dungeon in the books
of our day. And why not, do you think? Is there
less sin among us modern men, or did such writers
as John Bunyan overdraw and exaggerate the sinfulness of sin? Were they wrong in holding so fast
as they did hold that death and hell are the sure
wages of sin? Has divine justice become less fearful
than it used to be to those who rush against it, or
is it that we are so much better men? Is our faith
stronger and more victorious over doubt and fear?
Is it that our hope is better anchored? Whatever
the reason is, there can be no question but that we
walk in a liberty that our fathers did not always

walk in. Whether or no our liberty is not reckless-
ness and licentiousness is another matter. Whether
or no it would be a better sign of us if we were
better acquainted with doubt and dejection and
diffidence, and even despair, is a question it would
only do us good to put to ourselves. When we
properly attend to these matters we shall find out
that, the holier a man is, the more liable he is to
the assaults of doubt and fear and even despair.
We have whole psalms of despair, so deep was
David's sense of sin, so high were his views of God's
holiness and justice, and so full of diffidence was his
wounded heart. And David's Son, when our sin
was laid upon Him, felt the curse and the horror of
His state so much that His sweat was in drops of
blood, and His cry in the darkness was that His God
had forsaken Him. And when our spirits are
wounded with our sins, as the spirits of all God's
great saints have always been wounded, we too shall
feel ourselves more at home with David and with
Asaph, with Spira even, and with Bunyan. Despair
is not good, but it is infinitely better than indifference. 'It is a common saying,' says South, 'and
an observation in divinity, that where despair has
slain its thousands, presumption has slain its ten
thousands. The agonies of the former are indeed
more terrible, but the securities of the latter are far
more fatal.'

5. 'I will,' says Paul to Timothy, 'that men pray
everywhere, lifting up holy hands without doubting.'
And, just as Paul would have it, Christian and
Hopeful began to lift up their hands even in the
dungeon of Doubting Castle. 'Well,' we read, 'on

Saturday night about midnight they began to pray, and continued in prayer till almost break of day. Now, before it was day, good Christian, as one half amazed, broke out in this passionate speech: "What a fool," quoth he, "am I thus to lie in a stinking dungeon when I may as well walk at liberty; I have a key in my bosom, called Promise, that will, I am persuaded, open any lock in all Doubting Castle." Then said Hopeful: "That's good news, good brother; pluck it out of thy bosom and try."' Then Christian pulled the key out of his bosom and the bolt gave back, and Christian and Hopeful both came out, and you may be sure they were soon out of the giant's jurisdiction.

Now, I do not know that I can do better at this point, and in closing, than just to tell you about some of that bunch of keys that John Bunyan found from time to time in his own bosom, and which made all his prison doors one after another fly open at their touch. 'About ten o'clock one day, as I was walking under a hedge, full of sorrow and guilt, God knows, and bemoaning myself for my hard hap, suddenly this sentence bolted in upon me: The blood of Christ remits all guilt. Again, when I was fleeing from the face of God, for I did flee from His face, that is, my mind and spirit fled before Him; for by reason of His highness I could not endure; then would the text cry: Return unto Me; it would cry with a very great voice: Return unto me, for I have redeemed thee. And this would make me look over my shoulder behind me to see if I could discern that this God of grace did follow me with a pardon in His hand. Again, the next day, at evening, being under many fears, I went to seek the Lord, and as I prayed, I cried, with strong cries : O Lord, I beseech Thee, show me that Thou hast loved me with an everlasting love. I had no sooner said it but, with sweetness, this returned upon me as an echo or sounding-again, I have loved thee with an everlasting love. Now, I went to bed at quiet; also, when I awaked the next morning it was fresh upon my soul and I believed it. . . . Again, as I was then before the Lord, that Scripture fastened on my heart: O man, great is thy faith, even as if one had clapped me on the back as I was on my knees before God. . . . At another time I remember I was again much under this question: Whether the blood of Christ was sufficient to save my soul ? In which doubt I continued from morning till about seven or eight at night, and at last, when I was, as it were, quite worn out with fear, these words did sound suddenly within my heart : He is able. Methought this word *able* was spoke so loud unto me and gave such a justle to my fear and doubt as I never had all my life either before that or after. . . . Again, one morning, when I was at prayer and trembling under fear, that piece of a sentence dashed in upon me : My grace is sufficient. At this, methought : Oh, how good a thing it is for God to send His word ! . . . Again, one day as I was in a meeting of God's people, full of sadness and terror, for my fears were again strong upon me, and as I was thinking that my soul was never the better, these words did with great power suddenly break in upon me : My grace is sufficient for thee, My grace is sufficient for thee, three times together; and, oh! methought that every word was a mighty word unto me; as *My*, and *grace*, and *sufficient*, and *for thee*. These words were then, and sometimes still are, far bigger words than others are. Again, one day as I was passing in the field, and that, too, with some dashes in my conscience, suddenly this sentence fell upon my soul: Thy righteousness is in heaven. And methought withal I saw, with the eyes of my soul, Jesus Christ at God's right hand. I saw also, moreover, that it was not my good frame of heart that made my righteousness better, nor my bad frame that made my righteousness worse, for my righteousness was Jesus Christ Himself, the same yesterday, to-day, and for ever. . . . Again, oh, what did I see in that blessed sixth of John: Him that cometh to Me I will in nowise cast out. I should in those days often flounce toward that promise as horses do toward sound ground that yet stick in the mire. Oh! many a pull hath my heart had with Satan for this blessed sixth of John. . . . And, again, as I was thus in a muse, that Scripture also came with great power upon my spirit: Not by works of righteousness which we have done, but according to His mercy He saved us. Now was I got on high: I saw my self within the arms of Grace and Mercy, and though I was before afraid to think of a dying hour, yet now I cried: Let me die. Now death was lovely and beautiful in my sight; for I saw that we shall never live indeed till we be gone to the other world. Heirs of God, methought, heirs of God! God himself is the portion of His saints. This did sweetly revive my spirit, and help me to hope in

God; which when I had with comfort mused on a
while, that word fell with great weight upon my
mind : Oh Death, where is thy sting? Oh Grave,
where is thy victory? At this I became both well
in body and mind at once, for my sickness did
presently vanish, and I walked comfortably in my
work for God again.'

Such were some of the many keys by the use of
which God let John Bunyan so often out of despair
into full assurance and out of darkness into light.
Which of the promises have been of such help to
you? Over what Scriptures have you ever cried
out : Oh, how good a thing it is for God to send me
His word! Which are the biggest words in all the
Bible to you? To what promise did you ever flounce
as a horse flounces when he is sticking in the mire?
And has any word of God so made God your God
that even death itself, since it alone separates you
from His presence, is lovely and beautiful in your
eyes? Have you a cluster of such keys in your
bosom? If you have, take them all out to-night
and go over them again with thanksgiving before
you sleep.

XXIII

KNOWLEDGE

'I will give you pastors after Mine own heart, which shall feed
you with knowledge and understanding.'

HE Delectable Mountains rise out of
the heart of Immanuel's Land. This
fine range of far-rolling hills falls
away on the one side toward the
plain of Destruction, and on the
other side toward the land of Beulah and the
Celestial City, and the way to the Celestial City
runs like a bee-line over these well-watered
pastures. Standing on a clear day on the highest
peak of the Delectable Mountains, if you have good
eyes you can see the hill Difficulty in the far-back
distance with a perpetual mist clinging to its base
and climbing up its sides, which mist the shepherds
say to you rises all the year round off the Slough
of Despond, while, beyond that again the heavy
smoke of the city of Destruction and the town of
Stupidity shuts in the whole horizon. And then,
when you turn your back on all that, in favourable
states of the weather you can see here and there
the shimmer of that river over which there is no
bridge; and, then again, so high above the river
that it seems to be a city standing in heaven rather
than upon the earth, you will see the high towers

and shining palace roofs and broad battlements of the New Jerusalem itself. The two travellers should have spent the past three days among the sights of the Delectable Mountains ; and they would have done so had not the elder traveller misled the younger. But now that they were set free and fairly on the right road again, the way they had spent the past three days and three nights made the gardens and the orchards and the pastures that ran round the bottom and climbed up the sides of the Delectable Mountains delectable beyond all description to them.

Now, there were on the tops of those mountains certain shepherds feeding their flocks, and they stood by the highway side. The two travellers therefore went up to the shepherds, and leaning upon their staves (as is common with weary travellers when they stand to talk with any by the way), they asked : Whose delectable mountains are these ? and whose be the sheep that feed upon them? These mountains, replied the shepherds, are Immanuel's Land, and they are within sight of the city ; the sheep also are His, and He laid down His life for them. After some more talk like this by the wayside, the shepherds, being pleased with the pilgrims, looked very lovingly upon them and said : Welcome to the Delectable Mountains. The shepherds then, whose names were Knowledge, Experience, Watchful, and Sincere, took them by the hand to lead them to their tents, and made them partake of what was ready at present. They said, moreover : We would that you should stay with us a while to be acquainted with us, and yet more to solace yourselves with the cheer of these Delectable Mountains. Then the travellers told them they were content to stay; and so they went to rest that night because it was now very late. The four shepherds lived all summer-time in a lodge of tents well up among their sheep, while their wives and families had their homes all the year round in the land of Beulah. The four men formed a happy fraternity, and they worked among and watched over their Master's sheep with one united mind. What one of those shepherds could not so well do in the tent or in the fold or out on the hillside, some of the others better did. And what one of them could do to any perfection all the others by one consent left that to him to do. You would have thought that they were made by a perfect miracle to fit into one another, so harmoniously did they live and work together, and such was the bond of brotherly love that held them together. At the same time, there was one of the happy quaternity who, from his years on the hills, and his services in times of trial and danger, and one thing and another, fell always, and with the finest humility too, into the foremost place, and his name, as you have already heard, was Knowledge. Old Mr. Know-all the children in the villages below ran after him and named him as they clustered round his staff and hid in the great folds of his shepherd's coat.

Now, in all this John Bunyan speaks as a child to children; but, of such children as John Bunyan and his readers is the kingdom of heaven. My very youngest hearer here to-night knows quite well, or, at any rate, shrewdly suspects, that Knowledge was not a shepherd going about with his staff among woolly sheep; nor would the simplest-minded reader of John Bunyan's book go to seek the Delectable Mountains and Immanuel's Land in any geographer's atlas, or on any schoolroom map. Oh, no. I do not need to stop to tell the most guileless of my hearers that old Knowledge was not a shepherd whose sheep were four-footed creatures, but a minister of the gospel, whose sheep are men, women, and children. Nor are the Delectable Mountains any range of hills and valleys of grass and herbs in England or Scotland. The prophet Ezekiel calls them the mountains of Israel; but by that you all know that he had in his mind something far better than any earthly mountain. That prophet of Israel had in his mind the church of God with its synagogues and its sacraments, with all the grace and truth that all these things conveyed from God to the children of Israel. As David also sang in the twenty-third Psalm : ' The Lord is my Shepherd, I shall not want. He maketh me to lie down in green pastures; He leadeth me beside the still waters.'

Knowledge, then, is a minister; but every congregation has not such a minister set over it as Knowledge is. All our college-bred and ordained men are not ministers like Knowledge. This excellent minister takes his excellent name from his great talents and his great attainments. And while all his great talents are his Master's gift to him, his great attainments are all his own to lay out in his Master's service. To begin with, his Master had given His highly-favoured servant a good understanding and a good memory, and many good and suitable opportunities. Now, a good understanding is a grand endowment for a minister, and his ministerial office will all his days afford him opportunity for the best understanding he can bring to it. The Christian ministry, first and last, has had a noble roll of men of a strong understanding. The author of the book now open before us was a man of a strong understanding. John Bunyan had a fine imagination, with great gifts of eloquent, tender, and most heart-winning utterance, but in his case also all that was bottomed in a strong English understanding. Then, again, a good memory is indispensable to a minister of knowledge. You must be content to take a second, a third, or even a lower place still if your Master has withheld from you a good memory. Dr. Goodwin has a passage on this point that I have often turned up when I had again forgotten it. 'Thou mayest have a weak memory, perhaps, yet if it can and doth remember good things as well and better than other things, then it is a sanctified memory, and the defilement of thy memory is healed though the imperfection of it is not ; and, though thou art to be humbled for it as a misery, yet thou art not to be discouraged ; for God doth not hate thee for it, but pities thee ; and the like holds good and may be said as to the want of other like gifts.' You cannot be a man of a commanding knowledge anywhere, and you must be content to take a very subordinate and second place, even in the ministry, unless you have both a good understanding and a good memory ; but then, at the last day your Master will not call you and your congregation to an account for what He has not committed to your stewardship. And on that day that will be something. But not only must ministers of knowledge have a good mind and a good memory; they must also be the most industrious of men. Other men may squander and kill their time as they please, but a minister had as good kill himself at once out of the way of better men unless he is to hoard his hours like gold and jewels. He must read only the best books, and he must read them with the 'pain of attention.' He must read nothing that is not the best. He has not the time. And if he is poor and remote and has not many books, he will have Butler, and let him read Butler's Preface to his Sermons till he has it by heart. The best books are always few, and they must be read over and over again when other men are reading the 'great number of books and papers of amusement that come daily in their way, and which most perfectly fall in with their idle way of reading and considering things.' And, then, such a minister must store up what he reads, if not in a good memory, then in some other pigeon-hole that he has made for himself outside of himself, since his Master has not seen fit to furnish him with such a repository within himself. And, then, after all that,—for a good minister is not made yet,—understanding and memory and industry must all be sanctified by secret prayer many times every day, and then laid out every day in the instruction, impression, and comfort of his people. And, then, that privileged people will be as happy in possessing that man for their minister as the sheep of Immanuel's Land were in having Knowledge set over them for their shepherd. They will never look up without being fed. They will every Sabbath-day be led by green pastures and still waters. And when they sing of the mercies of the Lord to them and to their children, and forget not all His benefits, among the best of their benefits they will not forget to hold up and bless their minister.

But, then, there is, nowadays, so much sound knowledge to be gained, not to speak of so many books and papers of mere pastime and amusement, that it may well be asked by a young man who is to be a minister whether he is indeed called to be like that great student who took all knowledge for his province. Yes, indeed, he is. For, if the minister and interpreter of nature is to lay all possible knowledge under contribution, what must not the minister of Jesus Christ and the interpreter of Scripture and providence and experience and the human heart be able to make the sanctified use of? Yes, all kinds and all degrees of knowledge, to be called knowledge, belong by right and obligation to his office who is the minister and interpreter of Him Who made all things, Who is the Heir of all things, and by Whom all things consist. At the same time, since the human mind has its limits, and since human life has its limits, a minister of all men must make up his mind to limit himself to the best knowledge; the knowledge, that is, that chiefly concerns him,—the knowledge of God so far as God has made Himself known, and the knowledge of Christ. He must be a student of his Bible night and day and all his days. If he has not the strength of understanding and memory to read his Bible easily in the original Hebrew and Greek, let him all the

more make up for that by reading it the oftener and
the deeper in English. Let him not only read his
Bible deeply for his sermons and prayers, lectures
and addresses, let him do that all day every day of
the week, and then read it all night, and every
night of the week, for his own soul. Let every
minister know his Bible down to the bottom, and
with his Bible his own heart. He who so knows
his Bible and with it his own heart has almost books
enough. All else is but ostentatious apparatus.
When a minister has neither understanding nor
memory wherewith to feed his flock, let him look
deep enough into his Bible and into his own heart,
and then begin out of them to write and speak.
And, then, for the outside knowledge of the passing
day he will read the newspapers, and though he
gives up all the morning to the newspapers, and
returns to them again in the evening, his conscience
will not upbraid him if he reads as Jonathan
Edwards read the newsletters of his day,—to see how
the kingdom of heaven is prospering in the earth,
and to pray for its prosperity. And, then, by that
time, and when he has got that length, all other
kinds of knowledge will have fallen into its own
place, and will have taken its own proper proportion
of his time and his thought. He was a man of a great
understanding and a great memory and great industry who said that he had taken all knowledge
for his province. But he was a far wiser man who
said that knowledge is not our proper happiness.
Our province, he went on to say, is virtue and
religion, life and manners: the science of improving
the temper and making the heart better. This is

the field assigned us to cultivate : how much it has lain neglected is indeed astonishing.

Now, my brethren, two dangers, two simply terrible dangers, arise to every one of you out of all this matter of your ministers and their know-ledge. 1. The first danger is,—to be frank with you on this subject,—that you are yourselves so ignorant on all the matters that a minister has to do with, that you do not know one minister from another, a good minister from one who is really no minister at all. Now, I will put it to you, on what principle and for what reason did you choose your present minister, if, indeed, you did choose him ? Was it because you were assured by people you could trust that he was a minister of knowledge and knew his own business ? Or was it that when you went to worship with him for yourself you have not been able ever since to tear yourself away from him, nor has any one else been able to tear you away, though some have tried ? When you first came to the city, did you give, can you remember, some real anxiety, rising sometimes into prayer, as to who your mini-ster among so many ministers was to be ? Or did you choose him and your present seat in his church because of some real or supposed worldly interest of yours you thought you could further by taking your letter of introduction to him ? Had you heard while yet at home, had your father and mother talked of such things to you, that rich men, and men of place and power, political men and men high in society, sat in that church and took notice of who attended it and who did not ? Do you, down to this day, know one church from another so far as spiritual and soul-saving knowledge is concerned? Do you know that two big buildings, called churches, may stand in the same street, and have men, called ministers, carrying on certain services in them from week to week, and yet, for all the purposes for which Christ came and died and rose again and gave ministers to His church, these two churches and their ministers are farther asunder than the two poles? Do you understand what I am saying? Do you understand what I have been saying all night, or are you one of those of whom the prophet speaks in blame and in pity as being destroyed for lack of knowledge? Well, that is your first danger, that you are so ignorant, and as a consequence, so careless, as not to know one minister from another.

2. And your second danger in connection with your minister is, that you have, and may have long had, a good minister, but that you still remain yourself a bad man. My brethren, be you all sure of it, there is a special and a fearful danger in having a specially good minister. Think twice, and make up your mind well, before you call a specially good minister, or become a communicant, or even an adherent under a specially good minister. If two bad men go down together to the pit, and the one has had a good minister, as, God have mercy on us, sometimes happens, and the other has only had one who had the name of a minister, the evangelised reprobate will lie in a deeper bed in hell, and will spend a more remorseful eternity on it than will the other. No man among you, minister or no minister, good minister or bad, will be able to sin with impunity. But he who sins on and on after

good preaching will be beaten with many stripes.
'Woe unto thee, Chorazin! Woe unto thee, Beth-
saida! For if the mighty works which were done
in you had been done in Tyre and Sidon, they would
have repented long ago in sackcloth and ashes.
But I say unto you, it shall be more tolerable for
Tyre and Sidon at the day of judgment than for
you.' 'Thou that hast knowledge,' says a powerful
old preacher, 'canst not sin so cheap as another
that is ignorant. Places of much knowledge'—he
was preaching in the university pulpit of Oxford—
'and plentiful in the means of grace are dear places
for a man to sin in. To be drunken or unclean
after a powerful sermon, and after the Holy Ghost
has enlightened thee, is more than to have so
sinned twenty times before. Thou mightest have
sinned ten times more and been damned less. For
does not Jesus Christ the Judge say to thee, This
is thy condemnation, that so much light has come
to thee?' And, taking the then way of execution
as a sufficiently awful illustration, the old Oxford
Puritan goes on to say that to sin against light is
the highest step of the ladder before turning off.
And, again, that if there are worms in hell that
die not, it is surely gospel light that breeds them.

XXIV

EXPERIENCE

My heart had great experience.'—*The Preacher*.
' I will give them pastors after Mine own heart.'

EXPERIENCE, the excellent shepherd of the Delectable Mountains, had a brother in the army, and he was an equally excellent soldier. The two brothers—they were twin-brothers—had been brought up together till they were grown-up men in the same town of Mansoul. All the Experience family, indeed, had from time immemorial hailed from that populous and important town, and their family tree ran away back beyond the oldest extant history. The two brothers, while in all other things as like as two twin-brothers could be, at the same time very early in life began to exhibit very different talents and tastes and dispositions; till, when we meet with them in their full manhood, the one is a soldier in the army and the other a shepherd on the Delectable Mountains. The soldier-brother is thus described in one of the military histories of his day : ' A man of conduct and of valour, and a person prudent in matters. A comely person, moreover, well-spoken in negotiations, and very successful in undertakings. His colours were the white colours of Mansoul and his scutcheon was the dead lion and the dead bear.'

The shepherd-brother, on the other hand, is thus pictured out to us by one who has seen him. A traveller who has visited the Delectable Mountains, and has met and talked with the shepherds, thus describes Experience in his excellent itinerary : 'Knowledge,' he says, 'I found to be the sage of the company, spare in build, high of forehead, worn in age, and his tranquil gait touched with abstractedness. While Experience was more firmly knit in form and face, with a shrewd kindly eye and a happy readiness in his bearing, and all his hard-earned wisdom evidently on foot within him as a capability for work and for control.' This, then, was the second of the four shepherds, who fed Immanuel's sheep on the Delectable Mountains.

But here again to-night, and in the case of Experience, just as last Sabbath night and in the case of Knowledge, in all this John Bunyan speaks to children,—only the children here are the children of the kingdom of heaven. The veriest child who reads the Delectable Mountains begins to suspect before he is done that Knowledge and Experience are not after all two real and true shepherds going their rounds with their staves and their wallets and their wheeling dogs. Yes, though the little fellow cannot put his suspicions into proper words for you, all the same he has his suspicions that he is being deceived by you and your Sabbath book ; and, ten to one, from that sceptical day he will not read much more of John Bunyan till in after-life he takes up John Bunyan never for a single Sabbath again to lay him down. Yes, let the truth be told at once, Experience is simply a minister, and not a real shepherd at all; a minister of the gospel, a preacher, and a pastor; but, then, he is a preacher and a pastor of no ordinary kind, but of the selectest and very best kind.

1. Now, my brethren, to plunge at once out of the parable and into the interpretation, I observe, in the first place, that pastors who are indeed to be pastors after God's own heart have all to pass into their pastorate through the school of experience. Preaching after God's own heart, and pastoral work of the same divine pattern, cannot be taught in any other school than the school of experience. Poets may be born and not made, but not pastors nor preachers. Nay, do not all our best poets first learn in their sufferings what afterwards they teach us in their songs? At any rate, that is certainly the case with preachers and pastors. As my own old minister once said to me in a conversation on this very subject, ' Even God Himself cannot inspire an experience.' No. For if He could He would surely have done so in the case of His own Son, to Whom in the gift of the Holy Ghost He gave all that He could give and all that His Son could receive. But an experience cannot in the very nature of things be either bestowed on the one hand or received and appropriated on the other. An experience in the unalterable nature of the thing itself must be undergone. The Holy Ghost Himself after He has been bestowed and received has to be experimented upon, and taken into this and that need, trial, cross, and care of life. He is

not sent to spare us our experiences, but to carry us through them. And thus it is (to keep for a moment in sight of the highest illustration we have of this law of experience), thus it is, I say, that the apostle has it in his Epistle to the Hebrews that though Christ Himself were a Son, yet learned He obedience by the things that He suffered. And being by experience made perfect He then went on to do such and such things for us. Why, for instance, for one thing, why do you think was our Lord able to speak with such extraordinary point, impressiveness, and assurance about prayer; about the absolute necessity and certainty of secret, importunate, persevering prayer having, sooner or later, in one shape or other, and in the best possible shape, its answer? Why but because of His own experience? Why but because His own closet, hilltop, all-night, and up-before-the-day prayers had all been at last heard and better heard than He had been able to ask? We can quite well read between the lines in all our Lord's parables and in all the passages of His sermons about prayer. The unmistakable traces of otherwise untold enterprises and successes, agonies and victories of prayer, are to be seen in every such sermon of His. And so, in like manner, in all that He says to His disciples about the sweetness of submission, resignation, and self-denial, as also about the nourishment for His soul that He got out of every hard act of obedience, —and so on. There is running through all our Lord's doctrinal and homiletical teaching that note of reality and of certitude that can only come to any teaching out of the long and deep and intense experience of the teacher. And as the Master was, so are all His ministers. When I read, for instance, what William Law says about the heart-searching and heart-cleansing efficacy of intercessory prayer in the case of him who continues all his life so to pray, and carries such prayer through all the experiences and all the relationships of life, I do not need you to tell me where that great man of God made that great discovery. I know that he made it in his own closet, and on his own knees, and in his own evil heart. And so, also, when I come nearer home. Whenever I hear a single unconventional, immediate, penetrating, overawing petition or confession in a minister's pulpit prayer or in his family worship, I do not need to be told out of what prayer-book he took that. I know without his telling me that my minister has been, all unknown to me till now, at that same school of prayer to which his Master was put in the days of His flesh, and out of which He brought the experiences that He afterwards put into the Friend at midnight, and the Importunate widow, as also into the Egg and the scorpion, the Bread and the stone, the Knocking and the opening, the Seeking and the finding.

> His children thus most dear to Him,
> Their heavenly Father trains,
> Through all the hard experience led
> Of sorrows and of pains.

And if His children, then ten times more the tutors and governors of His children,—the pastors and the preachers He prepares for His people.

2. Again, though I will not put those two

collegiate shepherds against one another, yet, in order to bring out the whole truth on this matter, I will risk so far as to say that where we cannot have both Knowledge and Experience, by all means let us have Experience. Yes, I declare to you that if I were choosing a minister for myself, and could not have both the book-knowledge and the experience of the Christian life in one and the same man; and could not have two ministers, one with all the talents and another with all the experiences; I would say that, much as I like an able and learned sermon from an able and learned man, I would rather have less learning and more experience. And, then, no wonder that such pastors and preachers are few. For how costly must a thoroughly good minister's experience be to him! What a quantity and what a quality of experience is needed to take a raw, light-minded, ignorant, and self-satisfied youth and transform him into the pastor, the tried and trusted friend of the tempted, the sorrow-laden, and the shipwrecked hearts and lives in his congregation! What years and years of the selectest experiences are needed to teach the average divinity student to know himself, to track out and run to earth his own heart, and thus to lay open and read other men's hearts to their self-deceived owners in the light of his own. A matter, moreover, that he gets not one word of help toward in all his college curriculum. David was able to say in his old age that he fed the flock of God in Israel according to the integrity of his heart, and guided them by the skilfulness of his hands. But what years and years of shortcoming and failure in private and in public life lie behind that fine word 'integrity'! as also what stumbles and what blunders behind that other fine word 'skilfulness'! But, then, how a lightest touch of a preacher's own dear-bought experience skilfully let fall brightens up an obscure scripture! How it sends a thrill through a prayer! How it wings an arrow to the conscience! How it sheds abroad balm upon the heart! Let no minister, then, lose heart when he is sent back to the school of experience. He knows in theory that tribulation worketh patience, and patience experience, but it is not theory, but experience, that makes a minister after God's own heart. I sometimes wish that I may live to see a chair of Experimental Religion set up in all our colleges. I fear it is a dream, and that it must have been pronounced impracticable long ago by our wisest heads. Still, all the same, that does not prevent me from again and again indulging my dream. I indulge my fond dream again as often as I look back on my own tremendous mistakes in the management of my own personal and ministerial life, as well as sometimes see some signs of the same mistakes in some other ministers. In my dream for the Church of the future I see the programme of lectures in the Experimental Class and the accompanying examinations. I see the class library, and I envy the students. I am present at the weekly book-day, and at the periodical addresses delivered to the class by those town and country ministers who have been most skilful in their pastorate and most successful in the conversion and in the character of their people. And, unless I wholly deceive myself, I see, not all the class—that will never be till the millennium—but here and there twos and threes, and more men than that, who will throw their whole hearts into the work of such a class till they come out of the hall in experimental religion like Sir Proteus in the play :

> Their years but young, but their experience old,
> Their heads unmellowed, but their judgment ripe.

It is quite true, that, as my old minister shrewdly said to me, even the Holy Ghost cannot inspire an experience. No. But a class of genuine experimental divinity would surely help to foster and develop an experience. And, till the class is established, any student who has the heart for it may lay in the best of the class library for a few shillings. Mr. Thin will tell you that there is no literature that is such a drug in the market as the best books of Experimental Divinity. No wonder, then, that we make such slow and short way in the skilfulness, success, and acceptance of our preaching and our pastorate.

3. But, at the same time, my brethren, all your ministers' experience of personal religion will be lost upon you unless you are yourselves attending the same school. The salvation of the soul, you must understand, is not offered to ministers only. Ministers are not the only men who are, to begin with, dead in trespasses and sins. The Son of God did not die for ministers only. The Holy Ghost is not offered to ministers only. A clean, humble, holy heart is not to be the pursuit of ministers only. It is not to His ministers only that our Lord says, Take up My yoke and learn of Me. The daily cross

is not the opportunity of ministers only. It is not to ministers only that tribulation worketh patience, and patience experience, and experience hope. It was to all who had obtained like precious faith with their ministers that Peter issued this exhortation that they were to give all diligence to add to their faith virtue, and to virtue knowledge, and to knowledge temperance, and to temperance patience,—and so on. Now, my brethren, unless all that is on foot in yourselves, as well as in your ministers, then their progress in Christian experience will only every new Sabbath-day separate you and your ministers further and further away from one another. When a minister is really making progress himself in the life of religion that progress must come out, and ought to come out, both in his preaching and in his prayers. And, then, two results of all that will immediately begin to manifest themselves among his people. Some of his people will visibly, and still more will invisibly, make corresponding progress with their minister; while some others, alas! will fall off in interest, in understanding, and in sympathy till at last they drop off from his ministry altogether. That is an old law in the Church of God : 'like people like priest,' and 'like priest like people.' And while there are various influences at work retarding and perplexing the immediate operation of that law, at the same time, he who has eyes to see such things in a congregation and in a community will easily see Hosea's great law of congregational selection in operation every day. Like people gradually gravitate to like preachers. You will see, if you have the eyes, congregations gradually dissolving and gradually being consolidated again under that great law. You will see friendships and families even breaking up and flying into pieces; and, again, new families and new friendships being built up on that very same law. If you were to study the session books of our city congregations in the light of that law, you would get instruction. If you just studied who lifted their lines, and why; and, again, what other people came and left their lines, and why, you would get instruction. The shepherds in Israel did not need to hunt up and herd their flocks like the shepherds in Scotland. A shepherd on the mountains of Israel had nothing more to do than himself pass up into the pasture lands and then begin to sing a psalm or offer a prayer, when, in an instant, his proper sheep were all round about him. The sheep knew their own shepherd's voice, and they fled from the voice of a stranger. And so it is with a true preacher,—a preacher of experience, that is. His own people know no voice like his voice. He does not need to bribe and flatter and run after his people. He may have, he usually has, but few people as people go in our day, and the better the preacher sometimes the smaller the flock. It was so in our Master's case. The multitude followed after the loaves but they fled from the feeding doctrines, till He first tasted that dejection and that sense of defeat which so many of His best servants are fed on in this world. Still, as our Lord did not tune His pulpit to the taste of the loungers of Galilee, no more will a minister worth the name do anything else but press deeper and deeper into the depths of truth and life, till, as was the case

with his Master, his followers, though few, will
be all the more worth having. The Delectable
Mountains are wide and roomy. They roll far away
both before and behind. Immanuel's Land is a
large place, and their are many other shepherds
among those hills and valleys besides Knowledge
and Experience and Watchful and Sincere. And
each several shepherd has, on the whole, his own
sheep. Knowledge has his; Experience has his;
Watchful has his; and Sincere has his; and all
the other here unnamed shepherds have all theirs
also. For, always, like shepherd like sheep. Yes.
Hosea must have been something in Israel somewhat analogous to a session-clerk among ourselves.
'Like priest like people' is certainly a digest of
some such experience. Let some inquisitive beginner in Hebrew this winter search out the prophet
upon that matter, consulting Mr. Hutcheson and
Dr. Pusey, and he will let me hear the result.

4. Now, my brethren, in closing, we must all
keep it clearly before our minds, and that too every
day we live, that God orders and overrules this whole
world, and, indeed, keeps it going, very much just that
He may by means of it make unceasing experiment
upon His people. Experiment, you know, results
in experience. There is no other way by which
any man can attain to a religious experience but by
undergoing temptation, trial, tribulation :—experiment. And it gives a divine dignity to all things,
great and small, good and bad, when we see them
all taken up into God's hand, in order that by means
of them He may make for Himself an experienced
people. Human life on this earth, when viewed
under this aspect, is one vast workshop. And all

the shafts and wheels and pulleys; all the crushing hammers, and all the whirling knives; all the furnaces and smelting-pots; all the graving tools and smoothing irons, are all so many divinely-designed and divinely-worked instruments all directed in upon this one result,—our being deeply experienced in the ways of God till we are for ever fashioned into His nature and likeness. Our faith in the unseen world and in our unseen God and Saviour is at one time put to the experiment. At another time it is our love to Him; the reality of it, and the strength of it. At another time it is our submission and our resignation to His will. At another time it is our humility, or our meekness, or our capacity for self-denial, or our will and ability to forgive an injury, or our perseverance in still unanswered prayer; and so on the ever-shifting but never-ceasing experiment goes. I do beseech you, my brethren, take that true view of life home with you again this night. This true view of life, namely, that experience in the divine life can only come to you through your being much experimented upon. Meet all your trials and tribulations and temptations, then, under this assurance, that all things will work together for good to you also if you are only rightly exercised by means of them. Nothing else but this growing experience and this settling assurance will be able to support you under the sudden ills of life; but this will do it. This, when you begin by experience to see that all this life, and all the good and all the ill of this life, are all under this splendid divine law,— that your tribulations also are indeed working within you a patience, and your patience an experience, and your experience a hope that maketh not ashamed.

XXV

WATCHFUL

'Son of man, I have made thee a watchman unto the house of Israel.'—*The word of the Lord to Ezekiel.*

'They watch for your souls.'—*The Apostle to the Hebrews.*

THERE were four shepherds who had the care of Immanuel's sheep on the Delectable Mountains, and their names were Knowledge, Experience, Watchful, and Sincere. Now, in that very beautiful episode of his great allegory, John Bunyan is doing his very utmost to impress upon all his ministerial readers how much there is that goes to the making of a good minister, and how much every good minister has to do. Each several minister must do all that in him lies, from the day of his ordination to the day of his death, to be all to his people that those four shepherds were to Immanuel's sheep. He is to labour, in season and out of season, to be a minister of the ripest possible knowledge, the deepest and widest possible experience, the most sleepless watchfulness, and the most absolute and scrupulous sincerity. Now, enough has perhaps been said already about a minister's knowledge and his experience; enough, certainly, and more than enough for some of us to hope half to carry out; and, therefore, I shall at once go on to take up Watchful, and to supply, so far as I am able, the plainest possible interpretation of this part of Bunyan's parable.

1. Every true minister, then, watches, in the words of the apostle, for the souls of his people. An ordinary minister's everyday work embraces many duties and offers many opportunities, but through all his duties and through all his opportunities there runs this high and distinctive duty of watching for the souls of his people. A minister may be a great scholar, he may have taken all sacred learning for his province, he may be a profound and a scientific theologian, he may be an able church leader, he may be a universally consulted authority on ecclesiastical law, he may be a skilful and successful debater in church courts, he may even be a great pulpit orator, holding thousands entranced by his impassioned eloquence ; but a true successor of the prophets of the Old Testament and of the apostles of the New Testament he is not, unless he watches for the souls of men. All these endowments, and all these occupations, right and necessary as, in their own places, they all are,—great talents, great learning, great publicity, great popularity,—all tend, unless they are taken great care of, to lead their possessors away from all time for, and from all sympathy with, the watchfulness of the New Testament minister. Watching over a flock brings to you none of the exhilaration of authority and influence, none of the intoxication of publicity and applause. Your experiences are the quite opposite of all these things when you are watching over your flock. Your work among your flock is all done in distant and lonely places, on hillsides, among woods and thickets,

and in cloudy and dark days. You spend your strength among sick and dying and wandering sheep, among wolves and weasels, and what not, of that verminous kind. At the same time, all good pastors are not so obscure and forgotten as all that. Some exceptionally able and exceptionally devoted and self-forgetful men manage to combine both extremes of a minister's duties and opportunities in themselves. Our own Sir Henry Moncreiff was a pattern pastor. There was no better pastor in Edinburgh in his day than dear Sir Henry was; and yet, at the same time, everybody knows what an incomparable ecclesiastical casuist Sir Henry was. Mr. Moody, again, is a great preacher, preaching to tens of thousands of hearers at a time; but, at the same time, Mr. Moody is one of the most skilful and attentive pastors that ever took individual souls in hand and kept them over many years in mind. But these are completely exceptional men, and what I want to say to commonplace and limited and everyday men like myself is this, that watching for the souls of our people, one by one, day in and day out,—that, above everything else, that, and nothing else,—makes any man a pastor of the apostolic type. An able man may know all about the history, the habitat, the various species, the breeds, the diseases, and the prices of sheep, and yet be nothing at all of a true shepherd. And so may a minister.

2. Pastoral visitation, combined with personal dealing, is by far the best way of watching for souls. I well remember when I first began my ministry in this congregation, how much I was impressed with what one of the ablest and best of our then ministers

was reported to have testified on his deathbed. Calling back to his bedside a young minister who had come to see him, the dying man said: ' Prepare for the pulpit; above everything else you do, prepare for the pulpit. Let me again repeat it, should it at any time stand with you between visiting a deathbed and preparing for the pulpit, prepare for the pulpit.' I was immensely impressed with that dying injunction when it was repeated to me, but I have lived,—I do not say to put my preparation for the pulpit, such as it is, second to my more pastoral work in my week's thoughts, but—to put my visiting in the very front rank and beside my pulpit. ' We never were accustomed to much visiting,' said my elders to me in their solicitude for their young minister when he was first left alone with this whole charge; ' only appear in your own pulpit twice on Sabbath: keep as much at home as possible: we were never used to much visiting, and we do not look for it.' Well, that was most kindly intended; but it was much more kind than wise. For I have lived to learn that no congregation will continue to prosper, or, if other more consolidated and less exacting congregations, at any rate not this congregation, without constant pastoral attention. And remember, I do not complain of that. Far, far from that. For I am as sure as I am of anything connected with a minister's life, that a minister's own soul will prosper largely in the measure that the souls of his people prosper through his pastoral work. No preaching, even if it were as good preaching as the apostle's itself, can be left to make up for the neglect of pastoral visitation and personal inter-

course. 'I taught you from house to house,' says
Paul himself, when he was resigning the charge of
the church of Ephesus into the hands of the elders
of Ephesus. What would we ministers not give for
a descriptive report of an afternoon's house-to-house
visitation by the Apostle Paul! Now in a workshop, now at a sickbed, now with a Greek, now with
a Jew, and, in every case, not discussing politics and
cursing the weather, not living his holidays over
again and hearing of all the approaching marriages,
but testifying to all men in his own incomparably
winning and commanding way repentance toward
God and faith toward the Lord Jesus Christ. We
city ministers call out and complain that we have no
time to visit our people in their own houses; but
that is all subterfuge. If the whole truth were
told about the busiest of us, it is not so much want
of time as want of intention; it is want of set and
indomitable purpose to do it; it is want of method
and of regularity such as all business men must
have; and it is want, above all, of laying out every
hour of every day under the Great Taskmaster's eye.
Many country ministers again,—we, miserable men
that we are, are never happy or well placed,—complain continually that their people are so few, and
so scattered, and so ignorant, and so uninteresting,
and so unresponsive, that it is not worth their toil
to go up and down in remote places seeking after
them. It takes a whole day among bad roads and
wet bogs to visit a shepherd's wife and children,
and two or three bothies and paupers' hovels on the
way home. 'On the morrow,' so runs many an
entry in Thomas Boston's *Memoirs*, ' I visited the

sick, and spent the afternoon in visiting others, and found gross ignorance prevailing. Nothing but stupidity prevailed; till I saw that I had enough to do among my handful. I had another diet of catechising on Wednesday afternoon, and the discovery I made of the ignorance of God and of themselves made me the more satisfied with the smallness of my charge. . . . Twice a year I catechised the parish, and once a year I visited their families. My method of visitation was this. I made a particular application of my doctrine in the pulpit to the family, exhorted them all to lay all these things to heart, exhorted them also to secret prayer, supposing they kept family worship, urged their relative duties upon them,' etc. etc. And then at his leaving Ettrick, he writes: 'Thus I parted with a people whose hearts were knit to me and mine to them. The last three or four years had been much blessed, and had been made very comfortable to me, not in respect of my own handful only, but others of the countryside also.' Jonathan Edwards called Thomas Boston ' that truly great divine.' I am not such a judge of divinity as Jonathan Edwards was, but I always call Boston to myself that truly great pastor. But my lazy and deceitful heart says to me : No praise to Boston, for he lived and did his work in the quiet Forest of Ettrick. True, so he did. Well, then, look at the populous and busy town of Kidderminster. And let me keep continually before my abashed conscience that hardworking corpse Richard Baxter. Absolutely on the same page on which that dying man enters diseases and medicines enough to fill a doctor's diary after a whole day in an incurable hospital, that noble soul goes on to say : ' I preached before the wars twice each Lord's Day, but after the wars but once, and once every Thursday, besides occasional sermons. Every Thursday evening my neighbours that were most desirous, and had opportunity, met at my house. Two days every week my assistant and I myself took fourteen families between us for private catechising and conference ; he going through the parish, and the town coming to me. I first heard them recite the words of the Catechism, and then examined them about the sense, and lastly urged them, with all possible engaging reason and vehemency, to answerable affection and practice. If any of them were stalled through ignorance or bashfulness, I forbore to press them, but made them hearers, and turned all into instruction and exhortation. I spent about an hour with a family, and admitted no others to be present, lest bashfulness should make it burdensome, or any should talk of the weakness of others.' And then he tells how his people's necessity made him practise physic among them, till he would have twenty at his door at once. ' All these my employments were but my recreations, and, as it were, the work of my spare hours. For my writings were my chiefest daily labour. And blessed be the God of mercies that brought me from the grave and gave me, after wars and sickness, fourteen years' liberty in such sweet employment!' Let all ministers who would sit at home over a pipe and a newspaper with a quiet conscience keep Boston's *Memoirs* and Baxter's *Reliquiae* at arm's-length.

3. Our young communicants' classes, and still more, those private interviews that precede and finish up our young communicants' classes, are by far our best opportunities as pastors. I remember Dr. Moody Stuart telling me long ago that he had found his young communicants' classes to be the most fruitful opportunities of all his ministry ; as, also, next to them, times of baptism in families. And every minister who tries to be a minister at all after Dr. Moody Stuart's pattern, will tell you something of the same thing. They get at the opening history of their young people's hearts before their first communion. They make shorthand entries and secret memoranda at such a season like this : ' A. a rebuke to me. He had for long been astonished at me that I did not speak to him about his soul. B. traced his conversion to the singing of 'The sands of time are sinking' in this church last summer. C. was spoken to by a room-mate. D. was to be married, and she died. Of E. I have great hope. F., were she anywhere but at home, I would have great hopes of her,'—and so on. But, then, when a minister takes boldness to turn over the pages of his young communicants' roll for half a lifetime—ah me, ah me ! What was I doing to let that so promising communicant go so far astray, and I never to go after him ? And that other. And that other. And that other. Till we can read no more. O God of mercy, when Thou inquirest after blood, let me be hidden in the cleft of that Rock so deeply cleft for unwatchful ministers !

4. And then, as Dr. Joseph Parker says, who says everything so plainly and so powerfully : ' There

is pastoral preaching as well as pastoral visitation. There is pastoral preaching; rich revelation of divine truth; high, elevating treatment of the Christian mysteries; and he is the pastor to me who does not come to my house to drink and smoke and gossip and show his littleness, but who, out of a rich experience, meets me with God's word at every turn of my life, and speaks the something to me that I just at that moment want.' Let us not have less pastoral visitation in the time to come, but let us have more and more of such pastoral preaching.

5. But, my brethren, it is time for you, as John said to the elect lady and her children, to look to yourselves. The salvation of your soul is precious, and its salvation is such a task, such a battle, such a danger, and such a risk, that it will take all that your most watchful minister can do, and all that you can do yourself, and all that God can do for you, and yet your soul will scarcely be saved after all. You do not know what salvation is nor what it costs. You will not be saved in your sleep. You will not waken up at the last day and find yourself saved by the grace of God and you not know it. You will know it to your bitter cost before your soul is saved from sin and death. You and your minister too. And therefore it is that He Who is to judge your soul at last says to you, as much as He says it to any of His ministers, Watch! What I say unto one I say unto all, Watch. Watch and pray, lest you enter into temptation. Look to yourself, then, sinner. In Christ's name, look to yourself and watch yourself. You have no enemy to fear

but yourself. No one can hurt a hair of your head but yourself. Have you found that out? Have you found yourself out? Do you ever look in the direction of your own heart? Have you begun to watch what goes on in your own heart? What is it to you what goes on in the world around you compared with what goes on in the world within you? Look, then, to yourself. Watch, above all watching, yourself. Watch what it is that moves you to do this or that. Stop sometimes and ask yourself why you do such and such a thing. Did you ever hear of such a thing as a motive in a human heart? And did your minister, watching for your soul, ever tell you that your soul will be lost or saved, condemned or justified at the last day according to your motives? You never knew that! You were never told that by your minister! Miserable pair! What does he take up his Sabbaths with? And what leads you to waste your Sabbaths and your soul on such a stupid minister? But, shepherd or no shepherd, minister or no minister, look to yourself. Look to yourself when you lie down and when you rise up; when you go out and when you come in; when you are in the society of men and when you are alone with your own heart. Look to yourself when men praise you, and look to yourself when men blame you. Look to yourself when you sit down to eat and drink, and still more when you sit and speak about your absent brother. Look to yourself when you meet your enemy or your rival in the street, when you pass his house, or hear or read his name. Yes, you may well say so. At that rate a man's life would be all watching. So it would. And so it

must. And more than that, so it is with some men
not far from you who never told you how much you
have made them watch. Did you never know all
that till now? Were you never told that every
Christian man, I do not mean every communicant,
but every truly and sincerely and genuinely Christian man watches himself in that way? For as the
one essential and distinguishing mark of a New
Testament minister is not that he is an able man,
or a studious man, or an eloquent man, but that he
is a pastor and watches for souls, so it is the chiefest
and the best mark, and to himself the only safe and
infallible mark, that any man is a sincere and true
Christian man, that he watches himself always and
in all things looks first and last to himself.

XXVI

SINCERE

'In all things showing sincerity.'—*Paul to Titus.*

HARLES BENNETT has a delightful drawing of Sincere in Charles Kingsley's beautiful edition of *The Pilgrim's Progress*. You feel that you could look 'all day into those clear eyes. Your eyes would begin to quail before you had looked long into the fourth shepherd's deep eyes; but those eyes of his have no cause to quail under yours. This man has nothing to hide from you. He never had. He loves you, and his love to you is wholly without dissimulation. He absolutely and unreservedly means and intends by you and yours all that he has ever said to you and yours, and much more than he has ever been able to say. The owner of those deep blue eyes is as true to you when he is among your enemies as he is true to the truth itself when he is among your friends. Mark also the unobtrusive strength of his mouth, all suffused over as it is with a most winning and reassuring sweetness. The fourth shepherd of the Delectable Mountains is one of the very best of Bennett's excellent portraits. But Mr. Kerr Bain's pen-and-ink portrait of Sincere in his *People of the Pilgrimage* is even better than Bennett's excellent drawing. 'Sincere is softer in outline and feature than Watchful. His eye is full-open and lucid, with a face of mingled expressiveness and strength— a lovable, lowly, pure-spirited man—candid, considerate, willing, cheerful—not speaking many words, and never any but true words.' Happy sheep that have such a shepherd! Happy people! if only any people in the Church of Christ could have such a pastor.

It is surely too late, too late or too early, to begin to put tests to a minister's sincerity after he has been licensed and called and is now standing in the presence of his presbytery and surrounded with his congregation. It is a tremendous enough question to put to any man at any time: 'Are not zeal for the honour of God, love to Jesus Christ, and desire of saving souls your great motives and chief inducement to enter into the function of the holy ministry?' A man who does not understand what it is you are saying to him will just make the same bow to these awful words that he makes to all your other conventional questions. But the older he grows in his ministry, and the more he comes to discover the incurable plague of his own heart, and with that the whole meaning and full weight of your overwhelming words, the more will he shrink back from having such questions addressed to him. Fools will rush in where Moses and Isaiah and Jeremiah and Peter and Paul feared to set their foot. Paul was to be satisfied if only he was let do the work of a minister all his days and then was not at the end made a castaway. And yet, writing to the same church, Paul says that his sincerity

among them had been such that he could hold up
his ministerial life like spotless linen between the
eye of his conscience and the sun. But all that was
written and is to be read and understood as Paul's
ideal that he had honestly laboured after, rather
than as an actual attainment he had arrived at.
Great as Paul's attainments were in humility, in
purity of intention, and in simplicity and sincerity
of heart, yet the mind of Christ was not so given
even to His most gifted apostle, that he could
seriously say that he had attained to such utter
ingenuity, simplicity, disengagement from himself,
and surrender to Christ, as to be able to face the sun
with a spotless ministry. All he ever says at his
boldest and best on that great matter is to be read
in the light of his universal law of personal and
apostolic imperfection—Not that I have attained,
either am already perfect; but I follow after. And
blessed be God that this is all that He looks for
in any of His ministers, that they follow all their
days after a more and more godly sincerity. It was
the apostle's love of absolute sincerity,—and, especially, it was his bitter hatred of all the remaining
dregs of insincerity that he from time to time detected in his own heart,—it was this that gave him
his good conscience before a God of pity and compassion, truth and grace. And with something of
the same love of perfect sincerity, accompanied with
something of the same hatred of insincerity and of
ourselves on account of it, we, too, toward this same
God of pity and compassion, will hold up a conscience that would fain be a good conscience. And
till it is a good conscience we shall hold up with it

a broken heart. And that genuine love of all sincerity, and that equally genuine hatred of all remaining insincerity, will make all our ministerial work, as it made all Paul's apostolic work, not only acceptable, but will also make its very defects and defeats both acceptable and fruitful in the estimation and result of God. It so happens that I am reading for my own private purposes at this moment an old book of 1641, Drexilius *On a Right Intention*, and I cannot do better at this point than share with you the page I am just reading. 'Not to be too much troubled or daunted at any cross event,' he says, 'is the happy state of his mind who has entered on any enterprise with a pure and pious intention. That great apostle James gained no more than eight persons in all Spain when he was called to lay down his head under Herod's sword. And was not God ready to give the same reward to James as to those who converted kings and whole kingdoms? Surely He was. For God does not give His ministers a charge as to what they shall effect, but only as to what they shall intend to effect. Wherefore, when his art faileth a servant of God, when nothing goes forward, when everything turneth to his ruin, even when his hope is utterly void, he is scarce one whit troubled; for this, saith he to himself, is not in my power, but in God's power alone. I have done what I could. I have done what was fit for me to do. Fair and foul is all of God's disposing.'

And, then, this simplicity and purity of intention gives a minister that fine combination of candour and considerateness which we saw to exist together so harmoniously in the character of Sincere. Such a minister is not tongue-tied with sinister and selfish intentions. His sincerity toward God gives him a masterful position among his people. His words of rebuke and warning go straight to his people's consciences because they come straight out of his own conscience. His words are their own witness that he is neither fearing his people nor fawning upon his people in speaking to them. And, then, such candour prepares the way for the utmost considerateness when the proper time comes for considerateness. Such a minister is patient with the stupid, and even with the wicked and the injurious, because in all their stupidity and wickedness and injuriousness they have only injured and impoverished themselves. And if God is full of patience and pity for the ignorant and the evil and the out of the way, then His sincere-hearted minister is of all men the very man to carry the divine message of forgiveness and instruction to such sinners. Yes, Mr. Bain must have seen Sincere closely and in a clear light when he took down this fine feature of his character, that he is at once candid and considerate—with a whole face of mingled expressiveness and strength.

Writing about sincerity and a right intention in young ministers, old Drexilius says: 'When I turn to clergymen, I would have sighs and groans to speak for me.' For, alas! I am afraid that there be found some which come into the ministry, not that they may obtain a holy office in which to spend their life, but for worse ends. To enter the ministry with a naughty intention is to come straight to destruction. Let no minister think at any time of a better living, but only at all times of a holier life. Wherefore, O ministers and spiritual men, consider and take heed. There can be no safe guide to your office but a right, sincere, pure intention. Whosoever cometh to it with any other conduct or companion must either return to his former state of life, or here he shall certainly perish. . . . What is more commendable in a religious man than to be always in action and to be exercised one while in teaching the ignorant, another while in comforting such as are troubled in mind, sometimes in making sermons, and sometimes in admonishing the sick? But with what secret malignity doth a wrong intention insinuate itself into these very actions that are the most religious! For ofttimes we desire nothing else but to be doing. We desire to become public, not that we may profit many, but because we have not learned how to be private. We seek for divers employments, not that we may avoid idleness, but that we may come into people's knowledge. We despise a small number of hearers, and such as are poor, simple, and rustical, and let fly our endeavours at more eminent chairs, though not in apparent pursuit; all which is the plain argument of a corrupt intention. O ye that wait upon religion, O ministers of God, this is to sell most transcendent wares at a very low rate—nay, this is to cast them, and yourselves too, into the fire.'

There are some outstanding temptations to insincerity in some ministers that must be pointed out here. (1) Ministers with a warm rhetorical temperament are beset continually with the temptation to pile up false fire on the altar; to dilate, that is, both in their prayers and in their sermons, upon certain topics in a style that is full of insincerity. Ministers who have no real hold of divine things in themselves will yet fill their pulpit hour with the most florid and affecting pictures of sacred and even of evangelical things. This is what our shrewd and satirical people mean when they say of us that So-and-so has a great *sough* of the gospel in his preaching, but the *sough* only. (2) Another kindred temptation to even the best and truest of ministers is to make pulpit appeals about the evil of sin and the necessity of a holy life that they themselves do not feel and do not attempt to live up to. Butler has a terrible passage on the heart-hardening effects of making pictures of virtue and never trying to put those pictures into practice. And readers of Newman will remember his powerful application of this same temptation to literary men in his fine sermon on Unreal Words. (3) Another temptation is to affect an interest in our people and a sympathy with them that we do not in reality feel. All human life is full of this temptation to double-dealing and hypocrisy; but, then, it is large part of a minister's office to feel with and for his people, and to give the tenderest and the most sacred expression to that feeling. And, unless he is a man of a scrupulously sincere, true, and tender heart, his daily duties will soon develop him into a solemn hypocrite. And if he feels only for his own people, and for them only when they become and as long as they remain his own people, then his insincerity and imposture is only the more abominable in the sight of God.

(4) Archbishop Whately, with that strong English common sense and that cultivated clear-headedness that almost make him a writer of genius, points out a view of sincerity that it behoves ministers especially to cultivate in themselves. He tells us not only to act always according to our convictions, but also to see that our convictions are true and unbiassed convictions. It is a very superficial sincerity even when we actually believe what we profess to believe. But that is a far deeper and a far nobler sincerity which watches with a strict and severe jealousy over the formation of our beliefs and convictions. Ministers must, first for themselves and then for their people, live far deeper down than other men. They must be at home among the roots, not of actions only, but much more of convictions. We may act honestly enough out of our present convictions and principles, while, all the time, our convictions and our principles are vitiated at bottom by the selfish ground they ultimately stand in. Let ministers, then, to begin with, live deep down among the roots of their opinions and their beliefs. Let them not only flee from being consciously insincere and hypocritical men ; let them keep their eye like the eye of God continually on that deep ground of the soul where so many men unknown to themselves deceive themselves. And, thus exercised, they shall be able out of a deep and clean heart to rise far above that trimming and hedging and self-seeking and self-sheltering in disputed and unpopular questions which is such a temptation to all men, and is such a shame and scandal in a minister.

Now, my good friends, we have kept all this time to the fourth shepherd and to his noble name, but let us look in closing at some of his sheep,—that is to say, at ourselves. For is it not said in the prophet: Ye my flock, the flock of my pasture, are men, and I am your God, saith the Lord God. All, therefore, that has been said about the sincerity and insincerity of ministers is to be said equally of their people also in all their special and peculiar walks of life. Sincerity is as noble a virtue, and insincerity is as detestable a vice, in a doctor, or a lawyer, or a schoolmaster, or a merchant,—almost, if not altogether, as much so as in a minister. Your insincerity and hypocrisy in your daily intercourse with your friends and neighbours is a miserable enough state of mind, but at the root of all that there lies your radical insincerity toward God and your own soul. In his *Christian Perfection* William Law introduces his readers to a character called Julius, who goes regularly to prayers, and there confesses himself to be a miserable sinner who has no health in him ; and yet that same Julius cannot bear to be informed of any imperfection or suspected to be wanting in any kind or degree of virtue. Now, Law asks, can there be a stronger proof that Julius is wanting in the sincerity of his devotions ? Is it not as plain as anything can be that that man's confessions of sin are only words of course, a certain civility of sacred speech in which his heart has not a single atom of share ? Julius confesses himself to be in great weakness, corruption, disorder, and infirmity, and yet he is mortally angry with you if at any time you remotely and tenderly hint that he may be just a shade wrong in his opinions, or one hair's-breadth off what is square and correct in his actions. Look to yourself, Julius, and to your insincere heart. Look to yourself at all times, but above all other times at the times and in the places of your devotions. Ten to one, my hearer of to-night, you may never have thought of that before. And what would you think if you were told that this Sincere shepherd was appointed us for this evening's discourse, and that you were led up to this house, just that you might have your attention turned to your many miserable insincerities of all kinds, but especially to your so Julius-like devotions? 'And Nathan said unto David, Thou art the man. And David said unto Nathan, I have sinned against the Lord.'

What, then, my truly miserable fellow-sinner and fellow-worshipper, what are we to do? Am I to give up preaching altogether because I am continually carried on under the impulse of the pulpit far beyond both my attainments and my intentions? Am I to cease from public prayer altogether because when engaged in it I am compelled to utter words of contrition and confession and supplication that little agree with the everyday temper and sensibility of my soul? And am I wholly to eschew pastoral work because my heart is not so absolutely clean and simple and sincere toward all my own people and toward other ministers' people as it ought to be? No! Never! Never! Let me rather keep my heart of such earth and slag in the hottest place of temptation, and then, such humiliating discoveries as are there continually being made to me of myself will surely at last empty me of all self-righteousness and self-sufficiency, and make me at the end of my ministry, if not till then, the penitent pastor of a penitent people. And when thus penitent, then surely, also somewhat more sincere in my designs and intentions, if not even then in my attainments and performances.

'O Eternal God, Who hast made all things for man, and man for Thy glory, sanctify my body and my soul, my thoughts and my intentions, my words and my actions, that whatsoever I shall think or speak or do may be by me designed to the glory of Thy name. O God, turn my necessities into virtue, and the works of nature into the works of grace, by making them orderly, regular, temperate, subordinate, and profitable to ends beyond their own proper efficacy. And let no pride or self-seeking, no covetousness or revenge, no impure mixtures or unhandsome purposes, no little ends and low imaginations, pollute my spirit or unhallow any of my words or actions. But let my body be the servant of my spirit, and both soul and body servants of my Lord, that, doing all things for Thy glory here, I may be made a partaker of Thy glory hereafter; through Jesus Christ, my Lord. Amen.'